Dedication

I would like to dedicate   ok to my children and grandchildren. I want them to know what it was like for me growing up.

Acknowledgements

I would like to thank my Writer's Group who encouraged me to write. A big thanks to Marilyn Maun who directs the Writers Group and to Bonnie Keyserling who gave me much encouragement in the Writers Group.

A big thanks to Mary Jane Bryan who was born in Midland, Arkansas and knew some of the same people I grew up with in Midland, Arkansas. Thanks for her help and encouragement.

The biggest Thanks goes to my daughter who helped in the beginning with scanning pictures and to my son and daughter-in-law who helped with the computer and pictures. I owe my daughter-in-law a very big Thank You!

Last a very big Thank You to my husband, Jim who encouraged me to continue when I wanted to give up!

1

About the Author

I am Weda Faires Bailey married to Jimmie Ralph Bailey who also grew up at the Foot of Sugar Loaf Mountain.

We have two grown children, Adonis (our son) and Alethea (our daughter.) We have six grandchildren, two grandsons in laws and one granddaughter in law. We have two great grandsons Morgan James and Carter Joseph. These people are the love of my life. I am so proud of them for they have made a commitment to follow God.

This book started from a statement one of the grandchildren said. My husband and I were telling about something that happened while growing up. The statement was "Why don't you write this and other stories down that happened when you were growing up?"

These are just some of my memories I recall.

To my nieces, nephews and maybe my cousins, remember this is the memories I recall and how it affected me. Remember I'm writing how I remember, not how you remember or how it affected you. This is my first book to write.

I now live in Oak Grove, Missouri with my husband Jim, and our Goldendoodle dog, Teddy.

Chapter 1

At the Foot of Sugar Loaf Mountain

While growing up in Arkansas I always loved Sugar Loaf Mountain. I did not realize how much I loved it until I moved away. There are days now I wish I could wake up and see my mountain, which is how I always thought of it. We planned our day by the mountain. Upon arising early in the morning, dad or mom would say, "Clouds on the mountain, must be going to rain," or "Look at the ice on the mountain top," or "Look at the fog, can't even see the mountain."

A lot of Sunday afternoons were spent driving up the mountain road. It was a narrow and rough road with a gradual climb until you got to what is called "Lover's Leap." Some called Lover's Leap the First Cliff, which was a cliff of rock high on the mountain. You could look out and see Midland, a small town where my husband grew up and where we went to church, and other parts of the mountain. The cliff of rock hung out over the mountain and was flat enough that you could sit and have a picnic and enjoy the scene. Jim and I went to this cliff a lot while dating, and in later years after Jim had returned from serving eighteen months in Germany while in the Army, that was the first place we went with a picnic. You always took a quilt to sit on. My father-in- law said the original name was Roadside Bluff.

My father-in-law helped build the road up the mountain. He worked for W.P.A. This stood for the Worker's Progressive Administration, which was a government stimulus. Instead of giving money, they gave you jobs, plus commodities - which is food. This was started in the 30's during the depression.

You could keep driving from the first cliff to the top peak of the mountain. On the top peak, there was a lookout tower. It was kind of scary for the road up to the tower was real narrow and rough. Then there was a real sharp curve going to the left to get you on top of the mountain. The top of the mountain was small; not many cars could park there, and you hoped your brakes were good or off the mountain you went. Just before you reached the sharp curve there was a small white house on your left, the only house on the mountain. The house was built for the Forest Ranger, the person who worked in the tower. The Forest Ranger's job was to watch for fires or unusual happenings on the mountain. Two of the first Forest Rangers were Roy Oliver and Buster Bartlett.

The tower had lots of metal steps going up, then a trapdoor you'd go through. Then, you had to step to the side, so the door could be let down, so you could stand on it like a floor, for the space in the tower was very tiny. There was glass all around and the scene was beautiful, but I was like my mom, scared the whole time there. After I got married and was a little braver, my husband and I would go and stay longer to enjoy the scene, for it was beautiful. I was told the story of Smokey the Bear for the first time while I was in the tower.

While growing up I took the mountain for granted. When my kin folks came for a visit from Texas, they would stand on the porch with their coffee and admire the mountain. I thought they were crazy for in my mind I thought "It's just a mountain, let's get on with the day's work!"

After my husband and I married, we soon had to leave Arkansas and move to another state because of jobs.

At first life was an adventure for in my memory I did not remember living in any other state. I was born in Albuquerque, New Mexico. We moved to Arkansas when I was about two, so therefore I didn't remember.

It was not long after we moved away that I started missing the mountain and the country life. My husband and I had to live in town in those years. I then realized why my kinfolks loved looking at the mountain. We never got to move back close to the mountain.

My husband and I have been blessed living in different places and we've been very happy, and the Lord has blessed us. But we both feel that we are so blessed to have grown up at the foot of Sugar Loaf mountain and still have all those cherished memories.

Chapter 2

The Michael House

The summer I was four we moved into the Michael House. I woke up with my first earache. I remember crying and mom putting oil in my ear and holding me, trying to calm me down.

In the afternoon, mom and I laid down on the bed. We heard thunder, next hail stones started falling, hitting our tin roof. Now, I was really scared for I had never heard such a loud noise. I just knew the world was coming to an end. Mom put pillows over my ears to block the noise. I kept a tight hold onto mom.

When the storm was over, mom went out on the porch with me holding onto her dress tail. The whole yard was white with hail stones. Mom said, "Oh, if we hurry we can make ice cream!" Mom grabbed a wash tub and gave me one and said, "Hurry, gather the hail stones before they melt." Mom worked fast as she covered the hail stones with toe sacks -burlap sacks. She started mixing the ice cream mixture to put in the ice cream bucket. We packed the hail stones around it and we took turns turning the crank. Now this was a big deal during the middle of the week. It took extra money to buy enough block ice from the ice man to make ice cream.

Dad was surprised. He kept bragging on mom for her quick thinking. This could not be done every time it hailed, for there were not that many hail stones. This was a big hail storm and did a lot of damage to roofs and trees, including our roof. Dad had to put tar on all the holes for we had a tin roof.

As for my earache, it was better by night time. Dad said, "The hail stones had scared the earache away."

While living here I remember a dog named Tippy (he was black and white), and my brother Ray told me he came from a Doctor Linquist, who was a chiropractor that mom went to. Also for a short time we lived in his house that had a lot of farm land. Dad and doctor Linquist had made a deal for the doctor did not live there he lived in Fort Smith, Arkansas. He wanted someone to take care of the farm. We had moved here from Dardanelle, Arkansas.

Well we didn't live there long the deal didn't work out. That's when we moved to The Michael Place.

I remember playing with Tippy and I remember how I loved that dog. Now I don't remember who said it but someone in my hearing said, "a dog won't bite you unless you pull his tail and then he will bite you!"

One day while playing outside I was bored and did not want to go into the house for mom would find a job for me. I was playing with Tippy and I thought I'm just going to see if that's true, well I pulled his tail and he didn't bite. Then I decided I would pull harder and harder and sure enough Tippy bit me on my arm. It was three little teeth marks on my arm, I ran in the house and told mom "It's true if you pull a dog's tail hard enough he will bite you!" My mom went in panic mode, she went outside and put Tippy in the barn. I don't remember the details but the doctor or vet I don't know who said to shut Tippy up and watch him for mad dog disease (hydrophobia) and to watch me and my arm.

I cried and cried and told mom and dad it wasn't Tippy's fault, that I pulled his tail several times very hard. They would not believe me. I would sneak in the barn and talk to Tippy and tell him I was so sorry. Of course, in two weeks mom and dad knew he did not have mad dog disease, and I got slapped for I couldn't help but say "See I told you!" Now for the life of me I can't remember what happened to Tippy after that, because seems like I don't remember anything about him after that. I've wondered if they did get rid of him, and my brother and sister is not alive to ask for they remember the incident, they even talked to mom and dad to let Tippy out of the barn.

Weda – age 4

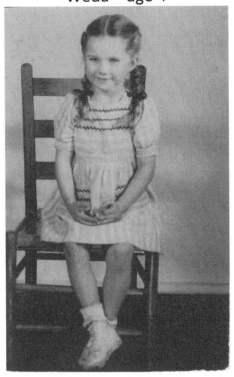

Picture of my family taken by Ray's friend
(one of the Michael boys)
Dad, Mom, me, Wanda and Ray Faires

The Faires Family (back) Virgil, Wanda, Ray,

(front) Grady, Weda, and Ethel Mae

I'll never forget this day, after our family

pictures we took Virgil to the bus station for he

was leaving for Guam.

I remember sitting by him and crying "Don't

go Bubba!" He pulled me close in tight squeezes

(which only Virgil did you would think he would crush your ribs.) He said I have something for you and he pulled out a package of juicy fruit gum from his shirt pocket, he said "Chew this and think of me coming back home soon!"

I had never had juicy fruit gum, and I thought it was so delicious. I held the rest of the package in my hand and when we got back home I put it in a safe place for I didn't want any one else to have any for that was my special gift from Virgil.

To this day I cannot chew a piece of juicy fruit gum without thinking of that day.

Chapter 3

Why Was I the Baby of the Family?

"And you think I had it easier being the baby?"

This was my reply to my brothers and sister when we were together after I was grown. I got so tired of my siblings saying, "You had it easier than we did. Mom and Dad changed by the time you came along."

Yes, I'm sure mom and dad changed by the time they had me, but something my siblings seem to forget is that I learned from their mistakes. I learned what upset mom and dad and I vowed I was not going to repeat what my siblings did that got them in trouble.

Also, I said, "Remember you are talking about a child who longed for her siblings' attention, but didn't understand why you were gone most of the time to school and the Army. "I was starving for your attention and mom and dad's, for their time was spent getting you all out of trouble! My troubles seemed like nothing, compared to yours, but to me they were big, like getting a sticker in my hand, my cat ran off, and being scared because you made mom cry and my dad being mad."

I do not know the whys or who was totally at fault, all I remember I was neglected in so many ways at a time when I needed it from mom and dad. They were always stressed out getting you guys out of trouble that I just got the leftovers."

One Christmas stands out to me when I was five. Mom and dad wanted to buy my brothers and sister a store-bought gift for Christmas that year. The reason being Virgil (my oldest brother) was in the Army now and the choice was made he join the Army or serve some jail time for drinking and fighting. He was being shipped out to Guam after Christmas, so mom and dad wanted to give him something special, which was a watch.

Rayford, my next brother, was in high school, he was quieter than Virgil, more of an introvert, but he got in trouble in a different way than Virgil. Rayford was sneaky, selfish and he knew mom would take care of him. Mom was partial to Ray for she worried about his health. When Ray was born the doctor said he had heart trouble and mom was to give him a spoonful of whiskey to stimulate his heart. As we found out later Ray outgrew his heart trouble but mom still worried, so she would give him the easier jobs and give him the lighter punishment. This caused trouble at times between mom and dad for I think dad could see the big picture. I think Ray played on this with mom which Virgil and Wanda (my sister could see) and it created jealousy toward Ray.

Well, Ray at this time seemed to be doing well and staying out of trouble, and he had decided he wanted to be a musician and learn to play the guitar. So, mom and dad bought him a guitar.

Wanda, my sister, was in high school just two years under Ray. She was pretty and very outgoing. Wanda was my dad's girl since birth.

My dad smoked cigarettes and a pipe Mom had tried to get him to stop, but she had no influence on dad. One day when Wanda was about five she was sitting on my dad's lap and dad was smoking. Smoke got in my sister's eyes and she said, "Daddy I wish you would quit smoking for that smoke hurts my eyes!" That day dad quit smoking, and never smoked again.

Wanda got in trouble a lot in high school, mainly flirting with the boys, and just enjoying life too much for a girl at that time. Since her and Ray had such different personalities her actions embarrassed Ray a lot. Wanda was gutsy enough that she could get even her teachers to like her even when she was doing wrong.

Well, at this Christmas mom and dad wanted to do something special for her for she had stayed out of trouble for a while. They bought her a jewelry box, a pretty brush and comb set, dusting powder and some other odds and ends that teenage girls like.

Mom came to me before Christmas that year and explained to me that they were really trying to come up with enough money to buy my older siblings store-bought gifts. Mom said, "I hope you don't mind, but we won't be able to buy you a store-bought gift for it's taking all that we have to get Virgil, Ray and Wanda their gifts". I think I started to tear up for I thought I was to get nothing. Mom said, "Oh honey you will be getting gifts but they will be homemade as usual, and I know you will understand."

Well, in my four-year-old mind I did not understand and for days I was sad about it. When Christmas came my siblings got their store-bought gifts and I got my homemade gifts. Mom and dad had worked at nights when I was asleep and made me several things. Mom made me my Raggedy Ann Doll which I got each year for the old one was wore out. She made me a stuffed elephant, a stuffed monkey, a stuffed cat and dad, who worked in the coal mines, brought home a wooden box that dynamite came in and made me a toy box. To this day I still have the toy box and used it for our son's toys when he was born. Now he is getting it for he is attached to it. Dad painted the ugly box black he wanted a different color, but light paint would not cover up the bold lettering on the box and he painted the inside red. He put rollers on the bottom, so I could move it around easily, then mom put all the stuffed toys in it for my Christmas present that year.

Now at first, I was a little resentful of my home-made gifts, but I couldn't stay that way long, for I did love my stuffed toys. Then when mom told me how her and dad stayed up at night working on my gifts at a time we had no electricity and they worked on the gifts by lamplight, I really began to appreciate my gifts.

There were many times I wondered, "why was I the baby of the family? Why was Virgil fourteen years older, Ray was twelve years older and Wanda was nine and a half years older?" Mom explained that she lost a baby boy that would have been two years older than me, born June 13th, 1941 and another baby boy was lost that would have been three years younger than me, born July 24th, 1946. Mom showed me their birth and death records in the Family Bible and we talked about it a lot. As time went by, when I would get sad that I had no one to play with, I would get the Bible out and look at the recordings of their births and deaths. I would even ask God "Why?"

My brothers and sister loved me their whole life, I knew it, but I also did not like how at different times in their life they made it hard on mom, dad and me. They made choices in their adult life that were not good, which caused them hurt and heartache.

Years after I was grown and married, they turned to me more and more, for I was the bright spot in their lives which at times were filled with troubles by their own choices. I tried to encourage them to stay strong and change some of their choices, but they had a way to justify their choices. At times it broke my heart, but I was so glad mom did not live to see this for it was better

my heart instead of hers.

Now I think I know why I was the baby of the

family? When I was a child it seemed unfair for I

didn't understand, but when I became an adult and

had my own family, my siblings turned to me and

would say "Let's ask little sis, or let's go see little

sis!"

Weda with homemade dolls

Weda at the age of four years

Weda at age of two years

Note- My brother, Ray left me some writings of his growing up. I did not fully read it until recently. I was shocked what my older siblings went through. Now I can understand why they said I had it easier, for I did.

First my parents were too hard on my siblings. They would get a whipping for everything and it was with the belt. Ray and Wanda could never understand why Virgil got the most licks with the belt when they were all doing the same thing. Some how they blamed Virgil for starting the trouble because he was the oldest.

Mom and dad moved so many times which hurt my siblings emotionally. From my brother's writing the best I could count they moved 33 times. This affected Virgil so that he would just get in trouble more. Ray missed one whole year of school from headaches which turned out to be emotional headaches from moving so much. My siblings would make friends at a school and start settling in the routine and dad would move again.

My sister got hurt for when we were at The Turner House she was enjoying high school, but she was sixteen at the age girls were interested in boys.

She was interested in this one boy and he in her, but she came in late one night and dad found out she was with a boy and he lost his temper.

I saw my dad beat my sister so hard, that she could not go to school the next day due to her bruises.   Then dad and mom pulled her out of school and sent her to live with some friends in Muskogee, Ok. This was against my sister's wishes she cried and cried and I did too.

She loved school and to my knowledge she never got to finish high school or get to come back home to live. That made me very sad and lonesome for now all my siblings were gone.

I wish I could have read some of this while they were alive, so I could talk to them about it.

My brothers (Virgil and Ray said they all loved me so much that they didn't want me to know.)

They knew I was having my struggles and mom and dad were still too strict. They all loved me so that they wanted to protect me.

Weda, Wanda, Ray & Virgil

Our last siblings picture together

Chapter 4

From a Tornado to Stinging Scorpions

Late one night my dad woke my sister, Wanda, and myself up and said "Hurry! Go to the other bedroom!"

He put us in bed with extra pillows and said, "Be Quiet!"

Dad was in his overalls with just his undershirt on, which was immodest for dad. Wanda and I knew something serious was up. The bedroom had windows facing the south from which you could see Sugarloaf Mountain. Dad and mom were standing in front of the windows looking out. By then, my sister and I had figured out there must be a storm coming. I'll never forget the feeling of how quiet it was. There was no thunder or lightning at the time. Then the molding that went around the ceiling suddenly buckled and fell across the bed. Wanda and I screamed.

Mom grabbed dad by his overall straps and said, "Let's get out of here!"

I'll never forget dad's answer, "It's too late now!"

It seemed like an hour as Wanda and I hugged each other with me crying, but I know it was just a few minutes. Dad said, "It's all over now. Come and listen." We all stepped out on the porch and we could hear a roar. Dad said, "the storm is moving down the hill away from us." Our house was on a hill and at the foot of Sugar Loaf Mountain.

Our chickens were running around in the yard making a lot of noise. The storm had blown their chicken house away, but not a feather was harmed. Our kitchen was destroyed. In the kitchen window mom had a sweet potato vine growing in a fruit jar, and the vine wasn't even disturbed. The window and everything else was gone, just the window seal left where the potato vine was. That storm was so spooky that I never forgot it and have had to fight the fear of storms all my life.

Dad was right. The storm went down the hill and tore up the house that we had lived in months earlier. It hurt my little girl friend who lived there at this time, but she got alright.

The house was damaged so badly that dad and my brother, Ray, who was in high school or had just finished, not sure memory wise here, had to look for us another place to live. Houses were hard to find. There was a lot of farm land and few houses and people didn't move a lot.

Ray heard of a house at the Murphy's Country Store. Mr. and Mrs. Turner, an elderly couple, lived in the house, but their daughter was moving them into town, close to her. This was the town of Midland, with only a population of three hundred.

The couple's last name was Turner, so we just called the house, The Turners' House. This house was located on two hundred and forty acres of coal mining land. There was a lot of coal in that area at that time. Coal companies would buy the land hoping to put mines on it. Not all land would have coal, so the coal company would lease their land for a dollar an acre. The lease would be for a year, so dad once a year had to pay two hundred and forty dollars.

The house was in bad shape. It had three rooms and a tiny room on the back. The land was so overgrown with brush right up to the house. Dad and my brother worked to clear out the brush with only an ax and a hand saw. They worked one day to clear the brush away from the house. We had to get moved into a house with a roof on before it rained. We moved in late that afternoon. My dad warned us not to go barefoot, for in cleaning the brush they had disturbed nests of stinging scorpions. The scorpions were crawling on the walls and on the floor.

My mom said, "We are not staying."

Dad said, "We have no other choice, there are no other houses." What a scary first night in our house. Dad made us all sleep with our bed sheet covering our whole body, for the scorpions were crawling on the ceiling and could fall on us. It was summer and very hot, so we sweated and jumped all night. There was no electricity in the house and no fans.

My brother did get stung on the arm and he said the sting felt like a hot needle. The sting swelled his arm up and he got sick. He stayed in bed off and on for a couple of days with mom doctoring the sting with poultices the chiropractor recommended.

Dad continued to clean out the brush. Someone told him to get some goats to eat all the underbrush from under the trees around our house. The chiropractor had already told mom she needed to drink goat's milk instead of cow's milk for her stomach troubles. The next endeavor was dad searching and buying goats.

In a year's time, the goats had eaten all the brush and the place was starting to look better.

During that year we continued to be jumpy and kill scorpions. It was lucky no one else got stung. The place started looking good and mom's stomach started feeling better.

Now you remember this was land in Arkansas. Some parts of the land were sandy, just right for scorpions. So, in all my growing up you had to always watch for scorpions. But watching for scorpions now and then is not the same as living in their nest, as dad would say, hearing them crawling on walls and ceilings at night.

I will never forget this experience from a tornado to stinging scorpions, in other words from bad to worse. Due to this experience at a young age I have always been afraid of storms and stinging scorpions. Also, goats became my favorite pets and friends. I grew up healthier by drinking goat's milk.

Chapter 5

The Turner House

The Turner House is the house we moved to after the tornado hit our last house. We called it the Turner House because the last people to live there, an elderly couple, was named Turner.

The house was in bad shape. The cracks in the wall were so wide you could see daylight. Dad told mom not to panic, he'd fix it. Dad went to all the stores and gathered up cardboard boxes, which were plentiful then. He flattened the boxes and tacked the cardboard to the walls. Mom papered the walls and ceilings with wallpaper. I didn't realize until later that the cardboard was like insulation. It made the house warm in winter.

Dad put up a warm morning stove. This was a wood-burning stove, but dad used coal, since he was a coal miner and he got the coal at a cheap price. Now the house was toasty. Some mornings dad would build too large of a fire in the stove. Mom would yell, "Grady, you are going to set the house on fire!" I can still see mom running her hand down the wall behind the stove and saying, "Dad this wall is hot—don't build such a big fire!" Dad did tell my sister and me, "Girls, if the house ever catches fire, *get out fast*, for this is a cardboard house!"

The house had a living room and a bedroom that was large enough to put two double-size beds in it. The kitchen was long and narrow and then there was a tiny room at the end of the kitchen. Mom squeezed a half bed in that tiny room. In later years when we had gas, mom put a tiny gas heater at the end of the room. We would come in from doing the chores and sit on a stool and warm our hands and feet.

Dad loved the open flame from the little heater. He would put his feet, with his still wet socks on, close to the flame and you could smell them scorching. Mom would call out, "Grady, you are going to set your feet on fire." Well, it happened one morning. Dad got his feet too close to the flame and his socks caught on fire. Dad started dancing around, yelling, "Ethel Mae, bring the water bucket!"

We had a nice front porch and a small back porch. Mom put some chairs and a rocker on the front porch. So many things happened on this porch. We would sit there and shell peas, beans and snap beans. Mom and I did the mending, piece quilts or embroidery dish towels and pillowcases. The front porch faced the east, so when the sun was high in the sky the porch would be in the shade from three large cedar trees.

In summer we would eat watermelon and homemade ice cream on the porch. That was usually when we had company. When it was just us, we'd eat the ice cream and watermelon on the back porch. Mom and dad together made the best ice cream. Mom practiced different recipes and finally came up with the one she liked and boy it was sure good. Then dad's part was beating the ice up in a toe sack(burlap) with his ax turned sideways. He learned when you first started turning the handle on the ice cream bucket you were to turn it slow. Which is opposite of what you want to do, then when the ice cream started freezing, you turned it faster which was hard. Dad then took the dasher out of the bucket and put the bucket back into ice, and it was to sit for at least an hour which helped firm up the ice cream. That was the best ice cream.

The back porch was not as large. On the north end of the porch my dad had built a shelf about waist high that would hold a water bucket with a dipper and a wash pan, bar of soap and a towel that hung on a nail for washing hands. We also washed our feet sitting on the back-porch steps, using the dish pan. This was done a lot in the summer for I went bare foot a lot, and our feet would get dirty working in the garden. Mom would let me wash her feet many times and she would sit, and rest and we would visit. As I look back I realize that was such a special time.

I would play after the canning, chores or whatever we were doing that day until dark. There were times I was so tired that I didn't want to wash my feet. So, I skipped one night. The next morning, I was in big trouble! Mom found out as we made the beds and saw the dirty spots on the sheets. At this time no one had colored sheets, the sheets were white, so dirty spots showed up easily.

The back porch was where we did the washing once a week, usually on Mondays unless it was raining. Mom had a wringer washer at last. Before the washer, she washed on a scrub board with a tub. There was a little while when we could afford it, mom drove to Hartford, Arkansas, eight 8 miles away, to a Laundromat – I'm not sure what it was called back then. The people that ran it was named Ford. They had twin girls my age, Lois and Doris. We went to high school together. We would play while mom did the washing. At that time, the washers were wringer type in the laundry mats, so it was still a lot of work.

Mom had two-bushel baskets lined with plastic just for the wet clothes. After washing we loaded up the wet clothes to go home and hang them on the line.

Mom had a special way you hung clothes on the line. You started at the end of the line with the large items, like sheets. Next line, at the end next to clothes line post, started with dad's overalls and mom's dresses. Then you went down to next smaller items. Men's underwear followed by socks and men's handkerchiefs. Same with women's clothes, their nightgowns, slips, panties, bras, socks and handkerchiefs. Towels started with large, smaller towels and washcloths. Dish towels same way, then dish rags and dust cloths.

We always had a lot of dish towels for all dishes were hand washed in a dish pan. There was no running water, so called if you did not have pipes ran to the inside of the house. Dad said that was not so. As he put it, "We ran to the well to get our water so that was running water." At the time dad thought that was funny but mom and I saw no humor in that.

Mom did all the garden canning in that small hot kitchen. The first years at The Turner House mom had a wood cook stove. Then dad ran some gas lines to the house and mom got a Home Comfort Gas Stove. I remember how excited my mom was, she danced all around in the kitchen. When mom got excited or happy about something she would dance around until her face got red. I loved it. I thought that was the whitest shiniest stove, for I was used to the black cook stove. A cook book came with the stove, it was called Home Comfort Cookbook.

Mom used the book a lot. At mom's death I was able to get the cook book. I still have it, but it is in bad shape from years of use and age. Mom loved cooking on that gas stove. Canning was easier instead of adjusting your temperature by how much wood you put in the stove, which was tricky, all mom had to do is just turn the knob.

Mom was a good gardener, she had two red wagons with bushel baskets that was used for the laundry. The vegetables were gathered and put in the baskets to be taken to the house or to the dug well to be washed.

We didn't have money, but with the milk from the cows and goats, eggs from the chickens, and vegetables from the garden, we had plenty to eat. Also, we raised chicken for meat, usually having young fryers, as we called them.

Some foods we fixed were varied. A lot of times at supper we had cornbread and milk. If you wanted something sweet, you put the cow's butter on the warm sliced corn bread and poured molasses over it and ate it like pancakes. We had wilted lettuce with bacon grease or just grease melted if out of bacon grease. The trick was to get the grease very hot or smoking as mom would say, then pour over the chopped lettuce. It was good with cornbread and garden onions and radishes.

Of course, everything was cooked in an iron skillet. By the way, if you wanted delicious fried chicken and still to this day, you fry the chicken in an iron skillet on a gas stove. The electric stove is harder to fry good chicken. Fried potatoes with onions chopped up in the potatoes.

Sometimes for breakfast we had mush, which was made with cornmeal and water. It was very hard for me to cook because at times, mine would turn out with lumps. Mom could make it the best and you could eat it warm with butter melting in the mush, or you could eat it like cereal with milk. Dad liked it like that, but I preferred mine with butter.

After we were able, and bought bread from the store, one of my favorite dishes was Toast and Gravy. Now I don't know if this was mom's creation or not, but I never heard of anyone else fixing it.

Mom would take the bread that was older in age and toast in the oven under the broiler. We didn't have a toaster. Then, in a large mixing bowl, she would tear the toast in bite-size pieces, the more toast torn the better. Next mom would pour just milk gravy, which is what we called gravy that was not made after frying chicken, over the bread and stir to get gravy on all the toast pieces. It was served immediately while it was while still warm because it tasted better that way. I loved it and still do, but it's too many carbs now that I'm older and not able to work it off.

This was a dish I made for our children, was a quick meal and very filling. Mom tried using biscuits instead of the store-bought bread, which is what it was called then when you bought bread from the store. Most women baked their own loaf bread. The biscuits did not work as well. Fried bologna or fried Spam was a favorite. Mom would buy it in the store telling the butcher how thick she wanted it. There was no packaged lunch meat then. Sad to say the meat was fresher then than it is now.

Mom was a good baker, she made cakes, pies, cobblers and fried pies. Mom encouraged me to bake cookies. Mom baked cookies, but she didn't think she was good at baking cookies. We all thought she was, and she inspired me to work on cookie making. I even started collecting cookie recipes. Because of mom's encouragement, I still like to bake cookies. Mom made chocolate pudding baked in the oven with meringue. I still can't bake a coconut cake as good as she did. At Easter she would make one and decorate it.

Just about every birthday I asked her to bake me a peanut butter layer cake. I never could find her recipe after she died, so it may have been one she remembered in her head. Other pies she baked were prune pie with meringue, raisin pie, mincemeat, lemon, coconut cream, chocolate, apple and cherry pie. The list could go on, because for mom even made up desserts using whatever ingredients she had.

Winter time after supper was one of my favorite times when mom wasn't so busy with the garden. Mom would play games with me, most of them were made up games. It was at this time she instilled in me the love of reading. Every night, she would read me a story out of Hurlbut's Story of the

Bible. As I got older she got me started on the Nancy Drew Mystery books.

We would pop popcorn in a pan on the stove shaking it to keep from burning. Sometimes we would parch peanuts in an iron skillet in the oven. You had to stir the peanuts often, so they would not burn. The popcorn and peanuts were the ones dad raised.

Dad would help me shell the peanuts. One night I said, "Dad, I think I can eat a whole skillet." "So, could I. How about we try?" he asked. We shelled and ate, shelled and ate until mom said, "Grady, you are going to make Weda sick and probably yourself."

Dad just laughed, but it wasn't funny in the middle of the night. I woke up with a stomach ache. I thought I was dying, then I threw up all those peanuts I had eaten. That was the first time I had thrown up and the only time I remember throwing up while a child. Mom was so mad at dad. It was a long time before I ate any more parched peanuts.

We only took a bath once a week on Saturday night. Early Saturday morning we would draw the water from the well and fill the tub that was put out in the open away from the shade of the trees. The sunshine would warm the water especially on hot days in summer.

At evening time, mom would heat water in

the tea kettle to add to it to make a little

warmer. We first only had the round wash tub to

bath in, you had to curl your legs up to sit in

it. Everyone bathed in the same water. Mom

would just warm the water up with more tea

kettles of water for each person. Our bath took

place on the back porch or under the shade of the

cedar tree that was close. When I was about

twelve, mom and dad bought a long, galvanized tub, that we used for a bath tub. Boy, that was awesome. You could stretch your legs out. In the winter time the tub was brought into the living room by the warm morning stove.

This house was small, but mom had made it cute with wallpaper and curtains she made. I grew up in this house and left the house when I got married. I have so many memories of this house and my mom that I could write a book within itself. Someday, I may write more about this house.

As I look back my earlier memories of childhood and growing to an adult all happened in this little house that we called The Turner House. I

did most of my growing up in this house, so it holds

a lot of memories for me.

Young Weda at The Turner House

Chapter 6

Canning Corn

"Mom, when will we ever get done canning this corn?" I asked plaintively. "I'm putting on the last cooker now, if you will wash up the pans, take the cobs to the pigs, you can have a break."

Canning corn is a messy job. You pick the corn, shuck it, flip the worms out and cut off the bad spots. You try to remove all the silk that you can, then wash the corn. Get sharp butcher knives, dish pans and large roasters. Start cutting just the top of the corn kernels. Next scrape the cob to make juicy cream corn, which was what we preferred.

Mom would heat the corn in a large dish pan with a little sugar and a little water if the corn was not juicy that year. You would have to stir the corn often, so it would not stick or scorch.

When heated, you would fill hot jars leaving more space at top than you did for other vegetables, for corn bubbles up more. Put lids on the jars that have been in hot water then the jar rings. Put in pressure cooker at 10 lb. pressure for forty-five to sixty minutes. I can't remember the exact time.

When time is up, you let the cooker cool down slowly. You must be careful when lifting corn out of the pressure cooker, for if you haven't let it cool down enough a jar could blow up and burn you.

Mom always taught us girls to keep our faces turned while lifting out. One of her friends didn't do that and a jar blew up in her face, burning her face badly.

Now I think you get the picture of why a young girl wanted a break from canning corn.

Years later, we got a freezer and it cut the time down a lot. No more pressuring, just put clean corn in boiling water for three minutes, then ice water until it was chilled even through the cob. Cut off corn as before, but put in freezer containers. We always put up several dozen ears of corn on the cob, which was easier

I hated the days we put up corn. I began to hate corn. But when winter came, and we were eating that good cream corn, I begin to forget the hard work. That was the best cream style corn!!!!!!

Today as I think of canning or freezing that corn, my mouth starts watering, and I think "YUM!" As my granddaughter would say "Yum, Yum!!!"

Finally, we got all pans washed, kitchen mopped, now it's off to the woods I'd go with Rusty by my side.

Chapter 7

The Trade

"Hurry, Weda, with your breakfast, or you'll miss the school bus."

As I stirred my thick, pasty oatmeal, wondering why a ten-year-old girl had to go to school, and looking at my big brother, Ray, I wished I were as old as he. Mother never made him eat oatmeal. The worse she would ever say to him was, "Did you shut the gate, Ray, so the cows won't get out."

Across the pasture, through the big trees, I saw the big yellow school bus. It was coming around the curve leaving a dust storm behind. I grabbed my books and lunch and ran to the barbed wire fence. Billy, my pet goat, was standing there.

"Ba a a a," I called to the goat.

Billy knew what I meant for we romped together every evening after school.

Finally, 4:00 p.m. arrived, and with a long day of school behind me, I was getting off the bus, hot, dirty and hungry. I ran into the house yelling, "Mother." But Mother was not in the house. I found some cookies and ran toward the barn to find Billy. "Billy, Billy," I called, but no Billy. I ran behind the barn stumbling over the chickens, looking, looking for Billy. "Now where could he be?" I finally decided he must have gotten hungry for grass and was off grazing with the cows, not realizing how late it was.

Walking slowly back to the house, I suddenly saw Ray coming. He had a look of excitement on his face.

"Hurry, Weda, I have something to show you!"

In the living room, my mother and dad were talking excitedly and examining a tall, black box, or that's what it looked like to me. I could not understand such excitement over such an ugly thing.

"Look what Ray got," my mother said.

"Well, what is it?" I said unenthusiastically.

"It's a Victrola," Ray said.

"A what?"

"Watch and listen" Ray said excitedly. He grabbed a handle which was on the side and wound it, like a jack-in-a-box. Then he opened a door and pulled out a record.

Suddenly to my amazement, music was flowing out of the Victrola. I watched the record go around and round, until I was dizzy. Ray even let me wind it up once. We played "Pop Goes the Weasel" and "They Cut Down the Old Pine Tree." Mother forgot to cook supper, and I forgot Billy, as we listened.

"Boy, I think I really got a bargain," Ray said.

"You sure did," my dad replied, "for not every day can you trade a Billy goat for a Victrola, plus all the records."

My heart froze...remembering Billy. A hurt was beginning in my stomach that I'd never felt before. I looked at them all, seeing a look of uncertainty in their eyes and realizing my Billy wasn't lost. I turned and took a last look at the Victrola before running out of the room, tears streaming down my face and calling "Billy...Billy...Billy...."

Picture of Billy

Chapter 8

Rusty

Not long after my brother, Ray, traded my Billy goat, he came home with a puppy. He told me he felt so bad about trading Billy that he got me a puppy. The puppy stole my heart immediately. It did help me get over the grief of Billy, for I was so busy with the puppy.

I named my puppy Rusty, for he was brown with white. Rusty was a mix breed of collie and bulldog. He had more collie but just enough bulldog to make him a fighter. Being a puppy, he got into everything. Dad would become harsh with him at times, but mother would say, "He just needs training."

At times, mother and I thought Rusty was too stubborn to train. I didn't care if he ever got trained, for I loved that dog and he loved me.

I would talk to Rusty like he was a person. "Rusty, please do what mom tells you or they will trade you off, too."

Rusty would lick my face and look at me with those brown eyes as if he was saying, "What are you talking about, I'm just doing what my nature tells me to do?"

Well, his nature told him:

1. To get the eggs out of the chicken's nest.

2. To attack and kill the young fryers.

3. To dig up mom's flowers.

4. To chase the young calves.

5. To jump up and grab the clothes hanging on the clothes line.

I was getting so concerned that I would lose him soon. But my mother loved him as much as I did. He had won mom over with his eyes and tail wagging. My mom then got as determined as Rusty.

One Sunday, when we came back from church, we saw two or more - can't remember -

dead chickens. These chickens we raised to eat as fryers. Rusty ran to meet us with feathers sticking out the sides of his mouth.

Dad said, "I'm going to shoot that dog." I started crying and mom said, "No, I will handle this." She shamed Rusty, then grabbed him by the back of the neck to drag him to the dead chickens. She picked up the dead chickens and while yelling "No, no, no," she whipped Rusty with the dead chickens, scolding him the whole time. She was worn out when she finished and not a dry thread on her, for it was summer time. Rusty tucked his tail and ran under the back porch. Every time he peeped his head out, mom would shame him.

The next incident was getting the eggs out of the nest. This time he didn't attack the chickens, just the eggs. Mom made a hole in some good eggs that Rusty hadn't touched and poured hot sauce and black pepper into the eggs. Once again, she got Rusty by the neck and forced his mouth open and made him eat the eggs. It was funny, for he ran around in circles foaming at the mouth and headed for the water bowl.

Now dad started to take interest in Rusty. "Ethel Mae, if you can train him to stay out of the chickens and eggs, then I'm going to try to teach him how to herd the cows." Dad had to first work on becoming friends with Rusty, which he did with mom's help. I don't remember the details of the training, but Rusty trained well in helping gather the cows to bring them to the barn. He seemed to love it when dad said, "Rusty, let's go get the cows!" Dad said that's the collie in him.

I was so happy now, for dad even liked Rusty and Rusty had learned to stay out of the chickens and the eggs.

Every day I would hug Rusty and say, "Now they won't trade you off like Billy." There was still an empty spot for Billy, but Rusty had helped fill that spot.

Things went along well until dad decided to raise rabbits, white ones. He worked for weeks building the rabbit hutches. Dad and mom had been gathering all the information on how to raise rabbits. They wanted to raise enough to kill and put in the freezer for meat, plus sell some.

Dad put the hutches under a big thorn tree by the barn. Now, why under a thorn tree where you would always have to wear shoes? Uncle Ruskin said, "Grady, you are crazy, now I will always have to wear shoes when I want to see the rabbits."

"Yes," Dad said, "No one will steal them because of the thorns, plus that thorn tree makes the largest shade."

That was true, it was a huge tree.

I visited the rabbit hutches a lot. They were white furry rabbits with pink eyes. I loved running my hands on the underneath floor of the hutches which was just wire. The rabbits would stomp their feet. I got into trouble for doing that. I couldn't wait until all the babies came, and I learned a lot about raising rabbits. I even wrote a paper in seventh grade for a school assignment.

I had to help shovel the rabbit manure which was put with the cow's manure for the garden. Both types of manure helped mom raise a good garden.

I did not like the day dad killed the young rabbits to put in the freezer. I had to help as I got older. Dad said I learned well how to dress out a rabbit, but it was a horrible day for me.

Rusty loved the rabbits and just like the chickens, he broke into a hutch while we were gone. He killed several young rabbits and ate one. Once again, mom did with the rabbits like she did the chickens. Rusty got beat with the two dead rabbits and once again he ran under the back porch and didn't stick his head out until the next day.

The amazing thing was, Rusty never killed another rabbit or chicken. When mom wanted to catch a hen for dinner, she would say "Rusty, that one!" and point. Rusty would run to the hen, catch the hen and sit on it or put his paws on the hen and hold it down until mom got there. Mom would brag on him and treat him. It was an amazing sight to see.

Rusty did the same with the rabbits, if one got out, which happened several times, he would catch it and lay his front legs and feet upon the rabbit, not letting it get up until mom got there and rescued the rabbit.

Rusty went from catching and eating chickens and rabbits to holding them for us. What a help he was.

When Rusty was about two years old, he got bit by a rattlesnake on his left paw. His paw swelled to three times its size with so much infection. Mom and I cried and cried, for we knew he would die. Mom had doctored him with all she knew, but he was getting worse and very sick, throwing up and wouldn't eat.

At this time mom went to an old country chiropractor, Doctor Henry. She told Doctor Henry about Rusty. Doctor Henry, being an animal lover, got involved in helping mom treat Rusty. He fixed mom poultices out of who knows what. He said the poultice would help draw out the snake's poison. Well, several weeks went by with mom putting the poultices on Rusty. This was one-time mom allowed Rusty to be in the house. At night, I sat up with Rusty encouraging him to drink water. I slept on a pallet, which is what we called a quilt on the floor, by Rusty's side, not sure for how many nights, but it was several. Dad was not very encouraging for he thought there was no hope and he just wanted to shoot him.

After weeks -not sure how many but I know it must have been close to three weeks - Rusty perked up. I got him to drink some water and mom I could tell the swelling in his foot was going down. Mom got some bread down him soaked in chicken broth. Mom and I were so happy, for you could see improvement in him each day.

Rusty didn't forget his experience with that rattlesnake, from then on, every time he even smelled a snake he would go in for the attack. What was amazing, he learned how to attack them without every getting bit again.

Rusty had another bad experience and that was with a snapping turtle. He was with dad helping bring in the cows. There was a wet-weather creek. This is what we called them in Arkansas. That's when the creek looks like a creek when it's rained a lot, but had no water in the creek bed during dry weather. There was a big snapping turtle by the creek and Rusty went in for the attack. The turtle clamped down on Rusty's nose and wouldn't let go. Dad said he tried everything to get the turtle to turn loose. Finally, he picked Rusty and the turtle up and put them in his old farm truck to come home.

We all worked all day to get the turtle to turn lose. Finally, about dark the turtle turned loose. By then, Rusty was so mad that the minute he was loose he went for another attack on the turtle. We all yelled "NO!" There was no stopping Rusty and he ended up and killed that turtle. He did have a sore nose for several days.

Rusty lived until I was sixteen. It was a sad day for mom and myself, for he was our life.

Dad had accidentally backed his truck over Rusty's back right leg while Rusty was asleep behind the truck. Dad didn't see him. Rusty's leg was hurt but you could tell it wasn't broken. The neighbor looked at Rusty and said the joint was probably crushed bad. Well, after a week, his leg swelled up in the joint. Dad would not take Rusty to the vet, although mom and I begged him.

"We don't have the money," Dad said. "But, Dad, you get the vet for the cows." "Yes, but that's our living. I can't afford to lose a cow."

Well, dad couldn't afford to lose a cow, but he didn't think about losing his daughter. I lost my respect and some love for dad that day. It was weeks before I spoke to my dad again. I know times were hard, but he had hurt mom and me so deeply. Months later I think dad realized it, but it was too late for Rusty. I was so sad, for not only had dad let Ray trade my Billy goat and now not getting the vet for Rusty. This confused me, for dad liked Rusty and used him a lot with the cows. I respected my dad as my dad, but I lost a closeness to him that I never regained. One thing I am thankful for, though, is the years I had with Rusty and the memories I still have of him. The memories of a girl and her dog!

Rusty

Rusty

Chapter 9

My Imaginary Friend

I was the baby of the family. There were four children living, two brothers and one sister. The brothers first in the family then my sister. Seven years after my sister was born my mom had a baby boy that died at birth. Two-and-one-half years later I was born. Three years later my mom had another baby boy that died at birth.

When mom showed me their birth dates written in her Bible, I became sad. I was probably around six. I would say "Oh my, how I wished they had lived for I would have two brothers close to my age to play with."

My sister was nine-and-one-half years older than me. Since they were that much older than me, they were gone most of my childhood. My oldest brother, Virgil, went into the Army. Ray, the next brother, went to college for a while then he joined the Air Force. My sister, Wanda, married young, she married a man that was in the Air Force. They never lived close while I was growing up.

This little girl was lonely for someone to play with.

My brother, Ray, who traded my goat, got me a puppy. I was thrilled, and the puppy took the place of my Billy Goat. I named him Rusty. He was brown with white spots.

I was so happy with my puppy and played with him and took him everywhere on the farm with me. My mother loved the puppy and helped me train him through the puppy stage.

Rusty wasn't enough; I wanted a friend that was not animal. I had a big imagination, so I decided I would have an imaginary friend.

I named her Georgia. When I played I always talked to Georgia? When I got in trouble I would go out into the woods and talk to Georgia. I would say "They don't understand."

There were times mom would call me in for supper, and I'd say, "I'll be there soon as I tell Georgia."

My childhood friend, Loreida, and her sister, Frieda, were over one day and we were playing house. I told them I had an imaginary friend, and they didn't even laugh. Frieda and Loreida said "Can we meet her and let her play in the play house with us?" That's what we did. If we were sitting the little table for us to pretend to eat we always added a place at the table for Georgia, with our toy dishes. We thought nothing of it and we continued to enjoy Georgia.

Now, being a child, I never thought about my mom getting worried over my friend Georgia. I also did not realize how much I was talking to Georgia all the time. When she first became my imaginary friend, I would just talk to her in the woods. As time went on I was talking to her all the time.

One day my sister, Wanda, was home for a visit. Wanda and my mom were washing the supper dishes, and I was outside feeding Rusty. I was always interested in what adults talked about. I knew it must be good for I was always told to leave when adults were talking. The windows were open for it was summer. After I finished feeding Rusty I snuck back to the kitchen window and squatted underneath it to listen to what mom and Wanda was talking about. My mother was saying "Wanda, I am so worried about Weda. I really think she is losing her mind. Could you observe her and watch her, for she is always talking to someone named Georgia?"

Wanda did watch me, but since I'd heard mom's conversation with her, I watched myself and did not talk to Georgia when Wanda was around.

Sometime later my sister confronted me about Georgia. Wanda said, "Weda, you need to stop the Georgia thing, for mom thinks you are off in the head." I just laughed and later in the day I had a conversation with my friend Georgia. "Georgia, my mom and sister thinks I'm going crazy, can you believe that?" I remember rolling in the grass with Rusty and laughing so hard and saying, "They think I'm crazy."

I was careful after that incident to watch who I was around when I talked to Georgia. It did not stop me, though. I continued with my imaginary friend. When I turned sixteen and started getting interested in boys and having a lot of girl friends in school, I decided it was time to tell Georgia, "Bye." I remember the day I talked to Georgia, I went to my favorite spot in the woods under a large dogwood tree with Rusty. I explained to Georgia how I was so busy with school and friends in school that it was time for us to part. I thanked Georgia for all the times she was there for me while I was growing up and lonely. I told

Georgia "You will always be in my heart and I will never forget you." I remember turning and leaving with Rusty by my side and waving good bye to Georgia with tears streaming down my face. I cried all the way home.

I was true to my word I never talked to Georgia again, but I always remembered her.

As I write this and think about it, I now begin to wonder like my mom - "Was I a little bit crazy?" No, I don't think so, I was just a lonely little girl with a big imagination.

Chapter 10

The Black Panther

It was in the early 1950's, when that part of the country had a drought. Now, it had stopped raining. Pasture lands were dead; there was no grass for the livestock. The wells were going dry and the pond had already dried up. Dad started hauling water in from wherever he could find it. We had one spring on the farm that supplied some water.

It was during this time that some of the farmers saw a lion. The farmers said, "I'm sure the lion came down from Sugar Loaf Mountain."

"Dad," I asked, "We do not have lions on the mountain?" My dad replied, "Sis (which he called me at times) we don't know what animals live on the mountain, for it's been years since it's been this dry. I've heard that people in the past have seen lions, bears and panthers."

Now panthers got my attention. I had two uncles - my mother's brothers - Uncle Bill and Uncle A. J., who told so many stories about panthers. My uncles, along with my grandpa, would play music for barn dances they had back then. My grandpa and my uncles grew up in East Texas. They did not have a car, so they would walk home after the dance very late at night. The road they walked on had a lot of trees hanging over the road. One night a panther had jumped on them as they went under a tree. My uncle A.J. had got scratched up bad, so they said. My uncles were good storytellers, so I know they embellished these stories some.

Uncle Bill and Uncle A.J. talked how awful a panther's scream was. My dad agreed with them saying "It will raise the hair on the back of your neck!"

Well, days went by with us hauling water for the farm animals, and I soon forgot about the lion someone had seen and my uncle's' stories.

Then one morning while I was on the school bus, just a few feet from our house and around a curve that was close to our house, the bus driver slowed the bus down and then stopped. "Look",

he said, and there in our pasture sat a big black

panther! When the bus got to school, the news

traveled fast throughout school. The teachers had

a hard time settling the students down to classes.

A week went by and everyone had settled

down, forgetting the panther.

Then one cold morning dad and I got up to

milk the cows and goats. Dad would milk the cows

and I would milk the goats. Dad got to the barn

first, and was already milking the first cow. I was

slowly making my way to the barn when there was

a loud scream. I had never heard such a loud

scream. The chickens ran into the chicken house,

all the farm animals stood very still and Rusty our

dog ran under the porch. Rusty would fight

anything. He even killed rattlesnakes, but this time

he ran. The cow dad was milking kicked the milk

bucket which was nearly full of milk and all the milk

went on dad. I ran for the house and met mom on

the back porch. I grabbed mom and hung on

tight. Everything became deathly quiet. No one

moved. Then we saw the panther running across

the pasture away from us. Mom started running to

the barn with me still holding on to her. Mom was

scared and worried about dad. When we got to the

barn we met dad coming out of the barn and he

was a funny sight. Milk was dripping off the bill of

his hat, his overalls and was wiping milk out of his

eyes. That broke the fearful tension. Mom started laughing and then everyone started laughing at the sight of dad.

My mom was short and on the plump side. No disrespect, but mom was like Santa Claus, when she laughed she shook all over and her face became very red. My mom's laugh was an infectious laugh, which made everyone join in.

By now all the animals were moving and Rusty had come out from under the porch. Dad then pointed to the trees and there was the big black panther again running across the pasture away from us.

We never heard another scream or saw him again. It had started raining at long last. Because of the rain the drought ended. Everyone knew then the lion and panther had gone back to the mountain where there was now food.

My Uncle Bill and Uncle A.J. were right about a panther's scream, it's a scream like no other, and will make the hairs rise on your neck. It's a scream I don't want to hear again.

Chapter 11

Christmas One Year

Mom had a good imagination which I think helped her survive when times were hard, and money was short.

The Christmas I was ten years old was a hard year money wise. The crops did not do good due to lack of rain. The price of beef was down. Sometimes dad would sell a cow to help us through the lean times.

It was three weeks before Christmas and dad made an announcement to mom and myself, that he was very sorry but there would be no Christmas this year because of lack of money.

Mom quickly said "No, we will have Christmas somehow." Mom then started singing "Here Comes Santa Claus, here comes Santa Claus," Of course, dad and I couldn't resist her joy so we all joined in the song.

The next day mom and I went into the woods with an ax. We found a big beautiful cedar tree.

"Mom, I said this is larger than we usually get."

"I know," she said, "but we are going to make this the best Christmas."

When we got back to the house hot and tired from dragging that large tree, our work really began. Dad, working in the coal mines, was doing a double shift that day. This meant he would work eight hours for the day shift, then turn around and work eight more hours for the night shift; he got more pay this way.

Mom said "Weda, we will have to fix the stand for the tree." This was always dad's job, which consisted of two boards cut in a plus sign and nailed to the bottom of the tree. Well, we worked and worked sawing pieces of wood with a hand saw - no skill saw in those days - and nailing it to the tree, but the tree always fell over. After a long time, mom's clothes were soaked in sweat.

She said, "I'll fix this tree, I'm going to nail it to the floor." I could not believe I heard mom right. Mom saw the look on my face and said, "Well, we always put the tree in the same spot every year, so when we take the tree down, I will just move the sofa down some to cover the nail holes in the floor."

Mom made me promise not to tell dad. So, we nailed the tree to the floor, and it did not wobble one bit. When dad came home he said, "Boy that tree looks nice." Dad went over and touched the tree and said, "How did you get it to be so stable? That's even better than when I do it." Mom just smiled and winked at me.

We continued to decorate the tree with icicles. You hung the icicles one at a time, so they would hang down. It was a long process. You never took a wad of icicles and threw them on the tree, but we were tempted to do so after hanging icicles for an hour.

That year, because of lack of money, mom's imagination went into overdrive. She said, "everyone will get one to two gifts under the tree." Mom looked at me. "Weda, we have a lot of work to do in a short amount of time."

That year, we sewed aprons from feed sacks, pot holders and dish towels from flour sacks. We made candy sweetened with molasses because for the last two years dad had put up a lot of molasses.

Dad grew sugar cane for the molasses. When the cane was ready, it was cut down, put on a wagon or the back of dad's truck and he hauled it to his neighbor, Fred McConnel, who was set up to make molasses. He had a horse tethered to a long pole attached to a grinder. The horse would walk circles all day grinding the juice from the long stalks of cane that was hand fed into the grinder. The juice was put in a large black pot with an open flame under it. Dad and Fred would take turns watching the liquid and keeping the top shimmed. It took hours before the molasses was ready to be put in jars or syrup buckets.

Everyone did get two presents. One gift was different kinds of homemade candy and the other gift was something handmade. The women and girls got aprons, pot holders, dishtowels, napkins, and the men got pajamas made from feed sacks, and shirts.

That three weeks before Christmas were the busiest days and nights. Yes, we had to work on our projects late at night when everyone was asleep and would not see what we were making.

That year was a Christmas I'll never forget. The surprise on everyone's faces when they opened their two gifts made all the effort worthwhile. The wonderment on their faces of how mom and I managed to cook the candy and finished all that sewing without them knowing about it or suspecting anything. After all the gifts were open, mom made us sing Christmas songs. It was also funny that mom and I had the same thought for each other. When mom thought I was making something for someone else, it was something for her. I made her an apron and embroidered her some dish towels. Mom made me a Raggedy Ann doll and a new dress. I know my mom must have stayed up all night to get my gifts done on time, for we worked together most nights.

It was a Christmas that stayed in everyone's memory and was talked about years and years later. It was a Christmas that taught me a lot of lessons. One was the lesson of how happy it made me see the look of surprise on faces. Another lesson that taught me that Christmas or any other time was not about me and what I received. Also, the lessons of making something out of nothing. I learned that all the hard work and late-night hours was worth it. That year I learned to appreciate mom more for all the hard work she did for her family. Yes, I wanted to quit many times, but mom kept pushing me and Christmas morning I was glad she did.

The best part of this Christmas was seeing the look on dad's face when mom showed him the nail holes in the floor where we nailed the Christmas Tree.

Years later, we heard someone saying to dad "Our Christmas tree keeps falling over." Dad just smiled and said, "Nail it to the floor."

Chapter 12

The Outhouse

The outhouse was also called a toilet. The toilet was what my family usually said. An outhouse or a toilet is a small building used for a bathroom. The toilet would have one or two holes for people to sit on when using the bathroom. There was no plumbing or electricity. Lime was used to cut down on the smell and to make it decompose faster and to cut down on the flies.

There was no soft Charmin bathroom tissue. The bathroom tissue was the Sears and

Roebuck, Montgomery Ward and National Bella Hess catalogs. This was a time when people got a lot of catalogs, for most people shopped ordering out of the catalogs. You would take a page out of the catalog and wad it up in your hands several times before use. Wadding it up makes it softer.

In the summer, I hated the toilet. First when opening the door, you had to check for spiders and snakes. Living in Arkansas we had black widow spiders. You didn't dare sit on the hole before looking just inside and around the hole, for that was a good place for a spider to hide.

Also, wasps could get inside and build a nest. In Arkansas, we had a lot of the big red wasps, and they would dive at you. When I got stung I would swell up bad and get fever, which meant I was allergic to them but did not find that out until after I had my kids and went to the doctor with a sting.

There's a lot of stories centered around the toilet. My big brother would sneak behind the toilet and with a tall bushy weed he had pulled he would tickle me on my bottom. I jumped and screamed and busted out of the toilet thinking I had been bitten by a spider.

The toilet was a good place to hide when playing hide and seek. My sister and I would hide there to get out of doing the dishes. Of course, mom caught on soon.

Since it was just a small, wooden building out back of the yard, made with cracks to help ventilate it, the toilet was hot to be in during the summer and very cold in the winter. Sometimes, if you had to get up in the night to use the bathroom, that was the scariest. I'd run to it and back, jumping on the back porch, skipping the steps. I just knew something would grab my legs from that dark space under the porch.

When it was real cold we had a chamber pot, or some people called them a slop jar. Our pot was white with a lid and you could push it under the bed. The next morning it was emptied to be ready for night.

It was a tradition that some of the toilets got pushed over on Halloween night.

When you mowed the yard, you always mowed the path to the toilet. I did not have an inside bathroom until I got married. I loved the inside bathroom, I could go to the bathroom without fear of snakes, spiders and wasps. I could take a bath in a large tub where you could stretch out your legs.

Now, I did miss looking at the catalogs. I would wish and dream for better things, or so I thought. But using bathroom tissue instead of the catalogs was the best. To replace the catalogs in the bathroom, I fixed a container to hold books to read. People complain about cleaning the bathroom, *NOT ME;* I'm thankful for my bathroom.

Chapter 13

Mail Carriers and Money Orders

In Arkansas, we called the mail person that delivered the mail to the mailbox, a mail carrier. Not every mail box was by your house. The mail carriers just went on the main dirt roads. If you did not live on a main dirt road, you put your mail box on the main road, no matter how far it was from your house.

Our mailbox was a quarter of a mile from the house. In the summer, it was my job to walk to the mailbox for the mail. The road was hot, sandy and dusty and I was always barefoot. Sometimes in the winter after I got in from school I would have to walk in the cold, snow, ice and freezing rain to get the mail.

We rarely went to town shopping; our shopping was done out of the Sears Catalog. After several days of looking at the catalog and seeing what we could afford, mom would make out the order. There were order forms in the catalog to use. Mom would then have to walk to the mailbox with her order and cash money to buy a money order from the mail carrier to send to Sears. The mail carriers carried money orders and money with them to be able to make change. They also carried stamps to buy.

I loved those days in summer when mom and I would walk to the mailbox to send off an order to Sears. Most of the time, we would walk together, and that was my time with mom. We always took a fruit jar wrapped in a dish towel filled with water and sometimes a snack to eat.

You never knew exactly when the mail carrier would arrive, so you made sure to leave early so you wouldn't miss him. At times, there was a lot of wait time. Mom and I would find a shade and drink our water and eat our snacks.

I enjoyed mom so much then, for she was away from the house and didn't see all the work that needed done. She was more relaxed, and we would talk and make plans and dream.

Now, I should mention that we usually carried a hoe or big stick with us. It was very common for snakes or big, black hairy tarantulas to be in the road. Now and then, we would have a mad dog show up. Most of the time you could tell the dog was mad because it would have bubbly saliva coming from its mouth, or what it was called then, foaming at the mouth.

When the mail carrier did arrive, not only did the money order get completed, but you heard a lot of news. Mom would ask "How are the Brocks?" or "I heard Mrs. Lovell was sick." The mail carrier was never on time for he was busy gathering news and passing it on. It was his time to visit and pass news on.

We would try to guess when our package would come and meet the mail carrier. If you missed meeting him on the day the package came, he would leave a note in the box. The next day mom and I would be there early. I've wondered if that's why I love getting packages today, even though I know what's in them, it still gives me a thrill.

One day, I was walking to the mailbox and a blue racer snake was in the road and I had forgot the hoe that day. The snake started chasing me, and I ran so fast back to the house and all the way to our big oak tree, where mom was washing greens to can. I grabbed mom and said, "A snake is after me!" She said "Where?" I looked behind me and the snake was not there. Mom believed me, for a blue racer had chased her before. At supper that night when we told dad, his response was, "Don't you know you don't run, instead turn around and start toward the snake like you are going to chase the snake and the snake will run off and leave you alone."

Mom and I both said, "Well we are *not* going to take that chance."

Chapter 14

Drawing water from a well,
Drinking out of a Dipper

When I grew up we did not have water in the house. We had to draw water from a well and carry it in buckets to the house. I never understood why everywhere we lived you went down a long incline with empty buckets to the well then up the long incline with full buckets of water to the house. Mother and I said it should have been reversed.

The well had two posts on either side and one across the top. The one across the top had a pulley in which the rope was threaded through and on one end of the rope was a bucket. It let the bucket down in the well to fill as it fell on its side, then you drew the full bucket up.

Now, we had two types of wells. One was a dug well, which was dug by hand until they found the stream of water. The well was wide, and round and the wall were fixed with rocks. Since the dug well was wider at the top it became dangerous for someone to fall in, so a pen was built around it and a lid to cover the well. The lid also helped to keep tree limbs, leaves, and animals from falling in the well. Our dug well had the coldest water. It was under a large oak tree, and there were surrounding trees which helped keep the well in a shade for most of the day. We would mow a big area around the well, so it was a shady place for me to play and mom to wash the garden vegetables.

Dad put a rope swing in the oak tree for me and that's where I spent most of my time when I was not busy with the chores or garden.

The other well was close to the barn. It was called a drilled well. It was done by a machine that was drilling to find gas on the land. If no gas was found, but they hit a good stream of water and the owner wanted a well, the gas company would put clay tile all around the hole for free. The hole was lot smaller than a dug well, probably about six inches across, so your bucket was long and narrow. It was easier for me to empty the water out of the dug well.

When dad was working hard in the garden, he would take a break and go to the shade of the oak tree and get a drink from the dug well. He would draw a bucket of water up and drink the water straight from the bucket and then throw the remainder of the water back into the well. This would make my mother so mad when she caught him.

"Grady, you are throwing your germs back into the well water!"

Dad would laugh and say, "Well, we all drink out of the same dipper, so what's the difference?"

"The difference," mom would reply "is you throw the water you don't drink from the dipper out in the yard!"

As I grew older and thought about this, there wasn't a lot of difference, for after all we did drink out of the same dipper.

Dad also put a cover over the drilled well that the rope went through, so you didn't have to manually take the lid off every time you drew water.

The dug well water was so much colder than the drilled well that we often put our milk in a gallon jar and put the jar in the well bucket and let down carefully until it just hit the water. This would keep the milk cold. We did not have

electricity.

Chapter 15

Muffy and Tuffy

I had two kittens named Muffy and Tuffy, which Tuffy is probably not a name but at ten years old what does it matter. I'll never forget the time Muffy ran down the well chasing a mouse. For some reason, the lid was off the well and a mouse came running out of the barn and ran up the tile of the well - the tile was about a foot above the hole - and into the well with Muffy right behind. Into the well they both went. I remember screaming! Mother was not far, and she thought I was hurt.

I cried hysterically, "Muffy is in the well, Muffy is in the well!"

Mom didn't believe me at first, then when she realized it must be so, she ran and got dad. I don't know where he was, but close enough, for we were doing the evening chores. Dad came running and he worked for a long time letting the bucket down into the well, hoping the cat was swimming and would grab onto the bucket. Muffy did grab the bucket after many tries, but half way up the bucket hit the wall of the well and scared Muffy and he jumped back into the water. Dad worked patiently and got Muffy back on the bucket and slowly, slowly pulled the bucket up and I was able to grab the cat. Mom went to the house with me and heated water to put a towel in to wrap around Muffy. Muffy was in shock, weak and shaking too weak to run. Mom heated some milk for Muffy to drink and that night mom let me keep Muffy in my bed, which was a "no-no."

Animals belonged outside.

That night I couldn't hug dad enough for saving my cat. He admitted, "Sis, I didn't think there was even a chance of getting that cat out of the well."

Mom said, "What about the mouse?" Dad said, "He'll just have to stay in the well." Mom said, "Don't anyone drink water out of that well for a long time." It was months before mom let us

drink out of that well.   Weda with Muffy

Muffy & Tuffy

Chapter 16

The Icebox

We did have an icebox. An icebox was commonly made from wood. The walls were lined with tin and packed with insulating materials like cork or sawdust. The block ice was held in a compartment at the top of the box. The bottom half was the storage compartment. Our icebox had a drip pan placed under the box and had to be emptied daily, which was mine and my sister's job. If we forgot we were in trouble, my sister thought she could excuse herself by telling mom, "Oh, don't worry, I will just mop the kitchen with this water."

That did not convince mom, for that was a job that was not done. An ice man would come around and you would buy block ice to put in the icebox. It would keep cold for a few days, if you didn't open the door that much. The ice man would come once or twice a week; I can't remember. You got a black and white card board sign - that was our color in Arkansas - that had numbers on each corner and the numbers were 25, 50, 75, and 100, this meaning how many pounds of ice you wanted. The ice was in 25-, 50-, 75- or l00-pound blocks. You put the sign in your screen door with the number up to what amount of ice you wanted.

The iceman had big tongs that would lift the ice off his truck and put in your icebox. If we were out in the garden or field, he would come in the house and leave the ice in the box. Mom would leave his money in a jar. You didn't lock your doors back then. I loved being at the house when he came for he would chip me off some ice with an ice pick. That ice was so good on a hot summer day. There was nothing better than drinking tea or lemonade with that chipped ice. We also made homemade ice cream with the block ice. Dad would put the block of ice in a toe sack (burlap sack) and beat it with the side of an ax to break up to put in the hand crank freezer with salt. Boy, that was the best ice cream.

When the ice all melted in the icebox we would put our milk and butter in the dug well to stay cool.

Chapter 17

Uncle Ruskin

Uncle Ruskin, Virgil and Ray

Uncle Ruskin, my dad's brother, lived in

Seagoville, Texas. Every summer he came with his

family to visit us for a week. Uncle Ruskin was a mail carrier.

Uncle Ruskin said he loved coming to the country, for he lived in the city with electricity and running water in the house when a lot of his folks were still like us. So, as I think of it, it's a wonder he would want to come to the farm for a vacation. Uncle Ruskin loved watching all the animals on the farm except the goats. He knew why dad got in the goat business because of mom's stomach problems, but he just learned to tolerate them.

Uncle Ruskin loved to drink fresh cow's milk and the churned butter mom made but he would always say, "Now, Ethel Mae, I do not have stomach trouble, so please do not give me goat's milk!"

While Uncle Ruskin was there mom and dad would make homemade ice cream with the hand cranked freezer and the block ice we got off the ice man. Uncle Ruskin would say, "Grady, don't put goat's milk in the ice cream." Dad would say, "Don't worry, I'm putting cow's milk in the ice cream" when all the time he was putting goat's milk in the ice cream. Now, goat's milk was a rich milk, for cream did not rise on it like cow's milk and it was naturally homogenized. Uncle Ruskin ate three bowls of ice cream and just kept bragging on how good it was.

Tongue in cheek, Dad said, "Yep, goat's milk makes the best ice cream."

"Oh no, you didn't, did you, Grady?" Uncle Ruskin was shocked.

Dad was laughing hard as he said, "I did!"

You had to have known Uncle Ruskin to appreciate this. At times, he left the impression that since he lived in the city and didn't have to work hard on the farm, he was just a little better than us. Yet mom and dad would laugh, for where did he come for a vacation in the summer. To the farm, of course, and sit on the front porch drinking his coffee and admiring Sugar Loaf Mountain.

I loved Uncle Ruskin, for he was very good to me. I had mixed emotions about Aunt Wilma Mae, his wife. At times, I liked her, but more times I didn't.

Aunt Wilma Mae wanted to live by a different standard than the rest of us in the family. She would always get new dresses at Easter and Christmas which were bought dresses. She bragged about it. If my mother and others in the family got new dresses they had to sew them.

I could tell at times that her attitude would get on Uncle Ruskin's nerves. He was always making excuses for her. At times, he would tell my mom, "Your dress is very pretty and it's special because you made it."

Uncle Ruskin told dad one time that he wished Wilma Mae was more like my mom. He had to spend so much money on her to buy everything she wanted. This was an era of time in that part of the country when money was tight, and women didn't ask for a lot.

Since childhood, I often wondered if Aunt Wilma Mae had a security problem. Aunt Wilma Mae had nothing to be ashamed of; she was a pretty woman and could be so loving at times.

Uncle Ruskin and Aunt Wilma Mae had two children, Judy and Larry. I tried to be nice to Judy and Larry, but they were so spoiled. They were a little younger than me but can't remember how much younger.

My toys were handmade, a Raggedy Ann doll and two or three stuffed animal toys like an elephant and a cat. Dad had made me a doll buggy and a wood wagon. I did have a yo-yo and jacks. Judy and Larry were not taught how to care for things or especially someone else's (that was a complaint I heard from the rest of the cousins). Many times, my toys would get broken or left out in the rain which messed up my stuffed toys.

Aunt Wilma would make them apologize but no offer to fix them or leave money.

Finally, mom got tired of hearing me cry so she went to dad with the problem. Mom wanting him to talk to his brother about this situation or discipline his kids. But Uncle Ruskin left the discipline to Aunt Wilma Mae for she would get mad at him if she thought he was too hard on the kids, and she would take the kid's side. Dad told mom he couldn't take the chance of ruining his relationship with his brother, who had enough problems with his wife.

So, mom solved the problem. When they came to the house mom would help me find hiding places to put my toys before they got there. Then she made during the winter when she had more time some stuffed animals out of feed sacks which was hurriedly made so were not the best of quality. That solved the problem for at least while they were young and hadn't caught on.

Every year at Christmas we would go to their house in Seagoville, Texas for the big family gathering. We always stayed at Grandpa and Grandma Faires' house. There were a few times we stayed at Aunt Zelma's house. This was dad's oldest sister who married my mom's uncle, who was Johnny Free. Mom and Uncle Johnny teased each other a lot about being kin in two ways. Aunt Zelma and Uncle Johnny had 8 children and they were so opposite from Uncle Ruskin and Aunt Wilma.

The adults drew names and the kids got presents from different ones. I don't remember how that was worked out.

The year I was eight years old, I think, I got my first store bought doll at that family gathering. Uncle Ruskin bought me the doll, it was a baby doll and came with a tiny bottle to be filled with water and wet its diaper. I was so happy, and I couldn't stop hugging Uncle Ruskin which brought tears to his eyes. When word traveled through the family about the doll it caused Uncle Ruskin some tension with Aunt Wilma Mae. Aunt Wilma thought it was too much money spent on my gift.

I'll never forget when I hugged Uncle Ruskin for my doll, he said, "I knew you would take care of this baby doll." So, the doll helped Uncle Ruskin and me both. I never forgot that moment and even after I was grown and had my kids when I'd see Uncle Ruskin I would hug him again and would tell everyone.

Uncle Ruskin bought my first store-bought doll.

Chapter 18

Loreida

I can still see Loreida, with orange-red hair, a freckled face, and very chubby. The summer we were eight, we built a playhouse under a big oak tree. Loreida would say, "I'm the mother." We'd fuss, and we'd end up both being mothers. If Loreida didn't get her desire to be the mother she'd throw her doll down, run to the house with her red hair bouncing. Tears would be streaming down her face making her freckles shine like new pennies.

Some summer afternoons we'd sit and daydream about having new dresses, new shoes, and money to travel to all the big cities. Loreida said she had an aunt that could provide these things we desired and daydreamed about them. She would say, "You just wait. She might come and get me any day to live with her, and I'll be wearing new dresses, new shoes and traveling."

I ran home and asked my mother if I had an aunts or kinfolk like Loreida's. I could picture in my mind Loreida wearing all those new clothes, and having money to spend, and me still in my faded feed sack dresses.

On some hot afternoons, we'd sit by the dusty road and wait, hoping the aunt would come that day. Loreida promised me that when she did come, she would share her new dresses. But if I didn't play the games Loreida wanted me to, she'd say, "Okay, I won't give you any new dresses."

Loreida's brothers would build us a little campfire in the park they had built for us. Loreida boiled potatoes in a coffee can and we'd eat the potatoes with salt, even though they were crunchy.

One hot day Loreida and I got in a fuss over our playhouse. She threw a mud pie at me. I threw a cup of water on her, and we both stamped home. I stayed in the barn loft and cried a lot, wishing we hadn't fussed. Mother kept asking me what happened, knowing we hadn't been together for two days. I finally told her, that we'd had a fuss. And guess what? I couldn't even remember what it started over. Mother told me to march over to Loreida's house and tell her I was sorry.

"No," I said.

Mother got a switch off a large cedar tree in our yard. I went, with Mother behind me, for she didn't want me to change my mind about going. When we were halfway down the road, we met Loreida and her mother. Loreida and I were so glad to see each other that we put our arms around each other. Both of us had tears running down our cheeks.

Loreida and I rode the school bus together, therefore, we were together some each day. I was her best friend at school the other kids made fun of her red hair and freckles. One time I found her sitting under a tree at recess crying. She would say, "I'll show them. When I grow up I'll be wearing new clothes, and I will be pretty like a princess, and I won't share with them. Then they will wish they hadn't made fun of my freckles and red hair."

We'd eat our sack lunches under the big trees on the playground. Sometimes I would trade my orange for Loreida's fried potato sandwich on a cold biscuit. It was tasty, for that was a sandwich I'd never eaten before. Loreida would peel the orange and eat it with juice running off her elbows, mixing in with her snotty nose. An orange was a real treat for Loreida, for she was in a family of ten and they couldn't afford oranges very often.

Summers came and passed. The summer we were twelve, Loreida's family moved. With tears in our eyes and a heavy feeling in our stomach, we waved goodbye. The activities of the past summer flashed in my mind: playing in the playhouse, playing in the park, and all the daydreaming we had done. I wondered what next summer would be like without Loreida.

Several years ago, I took our children to see the old oak tree where Loreida and I had our playhouse. It was still standing.

3 "stoogie" /

Freida, Weda and Loreida

Chapter 19

Adventures of Three Friends

"I'll race you two to the little curve and back, last one back is a rotten egg!"

My two friends, Barbara and David, were brother and sister. We played together a lot, Barbara was one year older than me and David was one year younger.

This time we were at their house which was in Midland, Arkansas. Their house sat on a hill with no other houses around them. There was a dirt road that started at the edge of their front yard. About 150 yards down the road was a curve which was called the little curve. There was a larger curve further down the road going toward town, these curves were called the big curve and the little curve. When you completed your turn around the small curve coming from town that's when the house came into view.

David had challenged Barbara and me. It was hot, and we were barefoot as always. No one wanted to be last in a dare and be called a rotten egg.

Away, we took off and we were all panting for breath time as we returned to the front porch. At different times, we all were a rotten egg.

We had a lot of adventures together. We were at each other's house a lot, our parents being friends was to our advantage.

We played church in the cemetery a lot. The cemetery called Mount Olive was close to Barbara and David's house. There was a shed for the graveside service, that is where we played church. It had a pulpit and some benches just like in a church building. David would be the preacher and we would take crackers and water for the communion. One day we had my niece, Linda, with us. We were supposed to be watching her, for she was about two years old, eight years younger than myself. Her mother, Tina, was at our house having a baby. Doctor Alvarez, the doctor from

Greenwood, Arkansas, would come to the houses and deliver babies. Suddenly, while David was preaching, he looked at Barbara and me and said, "The baby is supposed to cry, and you take the baby out!" "Why?" we asked. "Because that's what moms do at church when the baby cries." "But she's not crying," Barbara and I said. "Well, pinch her and make her cry." So, I pinched Linda and of course she started crying, so I got up and left our pretend church.

But poor Linda did not know why her Aunt Weda, who she trusted, pinched her and she would not stop crying.

We had to go to the house and have Barbara and David's mother calm her down. Mrs. Bailey asked, "What did you kids do to this poor child?" We told her innocent like, how we were playing church. "Oh, shaw, you kids beat all, you should be ashamed of yourselves!" I was afraid we would get a whipping, but no we were just to play around the house until my brother, Virgil, came for Linda and myself. Poor Linda just hung on to Mrs. Bailey's dress tail and would not let me touch her for a long time. I had broken her trust in me and I felt bad about it for a long time.

I was disappointed about Sandra, Linda's sister, who was born at my house. We kids thought the babies were in the doctor's black bag. We had already ruled out the storks bringing the babies, for

that was impossible. The babies would get wet or

cold for the storks flew in all kinds of weather. Now

this was a time when parents did not talk about

how babies got here.

When Virgil, Linda and I got back to our

house, the doctor was still inside the house with

Tina, my sister-in-law, and my mother. I heard the

doctor say he had to leave soon to deliver another

baby. The doctor's black bag was on the front porch

by the door. I thought the other baby was in that

bag and it was going to get too hot shut up in the

bag for it was a hot day in May. I looked around to

see if anybody was outside, then I quickly opened

the bag. What a surprise! There was no baby, only

doctor tools. I was so disappointed and mad, for I knew I hadn't been told the truth about babies.

Mother called me to come see my new niece. Tina (my sister-in-law) was laying in bed with the cutest baby laying by her. Tina looked at me, "What do you think we should name her?" I'll never know where this name came from but without hesitation I said. "Sandra is what we should name her." Tina said "What other name mother to go with it and mom said Faye. So, my little niece was named Sandra Faye and I loved her so much and was so happy I got to name her.

That Sunday at church I told Barbara and David the truth about the doctor's black bag. We still didn't know how Sandra got to my house, but she sure was cute.

We played hard in the summer - jumping in mud puddles and when it rained we would stand on the porch under the eve and see who could get the most water in our mouth.

We rode bicycles and rode double-head - meaning one riding on handlebars while the other pumped and steered the bicycle.

When trying to decide who would go first when starting a game, we used this rhyme to be fair:

Enie menie mighty mo

Catch a tiger by the toe,

If he hollers, make him pay

Fifty dollars every day,

Y-O-U, I choose you!

(As you say each word point to a different person.)

We played jump rope and many different versions of jump rope. We played Hot Pepper, throwing rope as fast as you can. You jumped in backwards with the rope being thrown toward you, which is hard.

We did a lot of jump rope rhymes:

Cinderella, dressed in yellow,

Went upstairs to kiss her fellow,

How many kisses did she get? 1,2,3,4,5...

until you missed a jump. The winner was the one

that got the highest number of kisses.

We caught lightning bugs to make diamond

rings, or put them in fruit jars to see if they would

light up in the house.

We played with locust shells and made pigs

out of large cucumbers by putting match sticks in

them for legs.

Barbara and David loved to fight wasp nests,

especially David. I wouldn't get as active in this

game for wasps scared me. If I got stung I would

swell up and have fever for days. In Arkansas, we

had the large red wasps, we also had dirt daubers which was like a wasp, but it didn't chase you like the red wasps to sting you. We would find their mud nest and tear them up, or sometimes on a hot summer day we would just lay on the porch and listen to their humming making their nest.

We played hop scotch, using small pieces of glass, from the trash pile, for markers.

We played jacks, marbles, or sometimes they were called doogies. Hop, skip and jump, mother, may I? I spy for a quiet game.

Many hours were spent on swings. My swing at my house was a rope swing hung from a large oak tree with a seat. Barbara and David's swing were a toe sack swing. A toe sack was stuffed with hay and tied at top, then tied onto the rope at top, you had to straddle it with your legs wrapped around it. Their swing was hung on a limb of a Catawba Tree, and to be able to go high you stood on a barrel and hopped on the swing and w-h-e-e-e! I never liked the toe sack swing like I did the rope swing, but Barbara and David could really swing on it and go high.

We played Annie Over. This is played with a ball. One person stands in front of the house and another person stands behind the house. The person in front of the house hollows "Annie." The person behind the house is to hollow "Over" which lets the person who is throwing the ball over the house know they are ready. Now, if that person catches the ball as it comes over the house that person is to quietly run around the house and tag the other person, if they can. If a tag is not possible then each person changes sides of the house and throws the ball over the house again. If a tag is possible then the person that tagged the other person with the ball gets a point. At the beginning of the game you decide how many points you are going to play for. It's a good game just for two people.

At dusk, we would watch for the first star to appear and make a wish, by saying this rhyme:

Star light, star bright,

First star I see tonight,

I wish I may I wish I might

Wish the wish I wish tonight.

Many nights we would see who could find the Big Dipper. My dad would do this a lot with me and would tell me to see if the dipper was holding water, or was it tilted so the water would run out, that meant it was going to rain. We could relate to the Big Dipper in the sky, for dippers were what we drank from. Without running water in the house, we drew water out of the well and filled the water bucket that sit on the porch or in the kitchen with a dipper in it for drinking when thirsty. Yes, we all did drink out of the same dipper.

Many times, we would explore the cemetery that was close to Barbara and David's house. There were times we would see a hobo, a homeless person walking from place to place. Sometimes the hobo would have a long stick over their shoulder with a bundle tied to the end, which would be his belongings or food which he got mostly by begging. At that time, you would often see one walking through the cemetery. We would run like wild horses to the house and jump on the porch, sliding into the porch wall for we were running so fast. Mrs. Bailey would yell "What are you kids up to now?" As kids, we were warned to run or stay away from a hobo, since they were wanderers, and no one knew what kind of person they might be.

We played in the barn loft a lot. We would sit and look down at the chickens and cows, and sometimes throw small rocks at the chickens just to see them run to the rocks thinking it was a bug to eat. One day, David and I were up in their barn loft. We got to talking about jumping out of the loft.

"I jump out of our barn loft all the time, but I think your barn loft is higher than my dad's," I said one time we were playing there.

"Oh no," David argued, "we jump out of it all the time!"

"Really? That ground looks too far away to me," I told him.

"I dare you to jump," David said.

Well, that did it. I jumped.

"Oh my!" I saw stars and my feet tingled all the way up my spine. Barbara and David rushed to me for I was sitting on the ground trying to recover. They were frightened, they both yelled "That's the first time ever anyone has jumped out!"

I looked at David and said, "You lied."

"I know, I know but I didn't think you'd take the dare and jump."

Years later, we talked about this incident. all of us remembering clearly even unto this day.

Most of the time we went to the same church at Midland, Arkansas. My mother taught our Bible class. We went home with each other a lot.

We had a lot of fun and adventures together.

As I look back and think about it, we had a lot of fun without a lot of toys or money. Those were such fun carefree days, but we didn't realize it at the time.

I also didn't realize that someday my two friends would become my sister-in-law and brother-in-law. I married their older brother,

Jimmie Ralph, who was five years older than me then later David married Linda, my niece, which made us kin in two ways, aunt, niece and sisters-in-law.

This picture was taken by my mother at our house one Sunday afternoon. I think Barbara was eleven years old, I was ten and David nine years of age. We were in our church clothes, but we did play in dresses that were usually made from feed sacks and usually we were barefoot.

(Barbara, Weda, and David)

Barbara and Weda

Some games we played:

Roly Holy: Played with marbles or doogies

Dig three holes in a vertical line. Dig another to the left or the third hole, it was called peggy. Starting at the starting line, making all four holes and continue to make them coming back to the starting line. After crossing the line, you were considered poison. Could go after anybody. Once you hit their marble with yours they were out of the game.

Jump Rope Rhyme: *Sing first verse of Skip to My Lou.*

> Next Ma made butter in Paw's old shoe,
> Ma made butter in Paw's old shoe,
> Ma made butter in Paw's old shoe,
> Skip to My Lou, my Darling
> Can't get a red bird, blue bird will do,
> Can't get a red bird, blue bird will do,

Can't get a red bird, blue bird will do,
Skip to My Lou, my Darling.

Lou, Lou, Skip to my Lou,
Lou, Lou, skip to my Lou,
Lou, Lou, skip to my Lou,
Skip to my Lou, my Darling.

Chapter 20

Going to school at midland

Mom and dad drove around Midland School House a lot of times to show me that's where I would go to school.

I would get excited for I loved the looks of the building and the large school yard with huge shade trees.

There was a rock wall about waist high on an adult where the buses would drop off the

Elementary students, then go on to Hartford (about 10 miles away) to drop off the high school students.

It was fun climbing the rock wall and walking on the top, but not so fun if you fell off and skinned your knees or hit your head.

I was scared to start school for I had not been around many children my age. The children in my Bible Class was all I had been around, plus mom taught that class.

Mom knowing this decided to start me a year younger, so I would be in first grade with Barbara Bailey (my Bible Class Friend.)

It was mainly left up to parents at what age a child started school.

There was no Kindergarten then, First Grade was the first year you started.

I was so excited to start school with Barbara.

School still turned out to be a struggle for

me. The teacher would slap your hands with a

ruler, which she did to me for not following instructions. I can't remember what it was, but I do know I didn't do it purposely, I was just too scared. I would look around the room and see all those kids at their desk and think, "I've never seen so many kids in my life."

Barbara tried to help me. She wasn't scared, and she made other friends quickly.

I cried every day and had a stomachache most of the time. I wouldn't eat my lunch. My sister liked that for she was going to high school at Hartford.

In the afternoon, the bus would pick up the high school students, first then to Midland to pick up the elementary students. My sister would be on the bus eagerly awaiting my leftovers from my lunch sack.

I don't remember how many weeks after school started that I came down with the measles. At that time, there was no vaccines for the measles.

I was sick for two weeks, which really put me behind in school. Mom wanted to send me back to school, but after talking to the teacher, she decided against it. The teacher said I was so young and immature. Now being behind so much with the school work, it would be too hard on me.

I was so happy! Mom reminded me that I'd have to go the next year, regardless. Well, a year in my mind was a long time.

To my disappointment, that next year rolled around. I was once again starting first grade. I was just as scared, but there was a different teacher in first grade now. She seemed to understand me and was not as strict. She gave me more hugs! That made it better, but I still couldn't learn to like school. I got the stomach ache when we were learning to print our letters.

I hated coloring, for I could not stay within the lines. My motor skills weren't developed fully so I colored outside the lines all the time.

I remember struggling with the little scissors in cutting out pictures.

Now, the glue topped everything. I would get too much on what I was gluing, too much on my desktop and all over me.

I know I was not reading as well as the other students. I would take my Dick and Jane book home for mom to help me. Those were our first reading books.

With mom's help I would do fine, but at school I couldn't read as well for the teacher.

I toughed it out that year and I think the teacher passed me on to second grade because she felt so sorry for me. I had more confidence when school started again. I was looking forward to second grade.

Mrs. Dalmont – Second Grade Teacher

Things went from bad to worse. Mrs. Dalmont was the second-grade teacher. She was petite, had dark hair and dark eyes. Mrs. Dalmont lacked organization and when she said to do something, you better do it, or she would stomp her feet and yell. All the students were in shock and a lot of parents complained.

To make matters worse, she would eat in front of us. This was in 1950 when money was scares our parents did not have money for extra treats, especially treats bought from the store. Treats like pop (what we called soft drinks in Arkansas.)

Mrs. Dalmont, about mid-morning would drink a coke, which was in a bottle, and eat a Snickers candy bar while she was checking our papers, leaning over our desks. Now, the coke didn't tempt me for I had never had one, but the coldness did, for you could see the frost or condensation on the bottle. Our room was hot; there was no air condition. The only air was from the windows that were open which at times were not much.

But the Snickers turned all of us on, our mouths would nearly drool when we smelled that chocolate, knowing it was candy which we students rarely got.

In the afternoon, she did the same thing, only instead of a Snickers she would have peanuts.

We all struggled that year. Looking back, I know this was a kind of emotional abuse to us kids.

For third grade, we had an older and more mature teacher, Mrs. Matthews. Third grade was combined with fourth grade. I liked that for my friend, Barbara, got to be in the same room with me. Mrs. Matthews would let the fourth graders help us out at times.

Mrs. Matthews was a teacher that you liked for she treated you fairly with no yelling, but at the same time you didn't love her. She was married but she didn't have children. I wasn't afraid of her, for she would help me with my assignments and I started to want to learn.

One day when she blew the whistle for us to come in from recess, the students were to line up in front of the school's front steps according to grades, then go in quietly when your teacher motioned your class to go. Well, I missed a step, fell and hit my chin on the next step. I guess my tooth cut my lip and blood started flowing. I immediately started crying, for the sight of blood scared me. Suddenly, Mrs. Matthews was there and carried me inside the classroom. She wiped the blood and put me in her lap and with her arms around me calmed me down.

Well, that was a side I didn't know Mrs. Matthews had and I fell in love with her that day.

It wasn't long after that incident my dad decided we'd move to Siloam Springs, Arkansas to run a dairy. Dad had been without work for a while. Progressive Farmer was a magazine about farming that we received, and dad and mom saw the add about the dairy in that magazine. Dad got the job, but our house was still under lease and we still had the cows, goats and chickens. Virgil, my oldest brother, lived close, so he was going to watch after the farm until dad knew for sure if this dairy job would work out. I was so sad for I was just now getting secure in school and had a lot of friends by now.

It was awful! I did not like the new school or the teacher. The teacher tried to be nice, but she knew I was very homesick for my old school and friends.

Dad's job wasn't working out too well. We had a very small house to live in which was part of dad's wages. The house was only two rooms, and a very small rocky yard on a hill, without my dog or cats which was left in my brother's care.

That winter was so cold. At Christmas, my two older brothers and my sister came. Mom must have told them how sad I was, for mom later told me she was very worried about me. They brought me more presents than I know they could afford. My oldest brother gave me a big stuffed poodle that was purple. My sister gave me a little black and white teddy bear, which I still have and my first New Testament, which now is not in too good a shape. My other brother gave me my first Mother Goose book, it was big, and the cover was yellow with a picture of Mother Goose. I still have it, but it also is in poor shape from usage and age.

Dad toughed out the new job for nearly three months (I think.) The dairyman didn't do as promised and we nearly starved to death. Dad said we can do better than this back home. Also, my older brother said he had found him a job.

I was so excited to get back to my old school. I remember Mrs. Matthews hugged me with tears in her eyes. Now, this was the second time that I really loved her.

My parents talked to her about how I was behind in my school work, for I was so homesick while we lived in Siloam Springs. The teacher from Siloam wrote a nice note with my report cards saying, "Weda didn't do good, because she was so homesick. I couldn't get her to love me like she did you. I wanted her to, so she could be happy."

I didn't appreciate this until I got older and I realized this teacher really cared for me.

Mrs. Matthews told mom she would stay after school herself - which was unheard of then - to help me catch up. I also had an advantage, for I would have Mrs. Matthews in the fourth grade.

Fourth grade went well. At the end of fourth grade Mrs. Matthews assured us that fifth grade would be fine. She told us that we would have a new teacher. She meant new in the sense that she had never taught at Midland, so she was new to everyone.

Mrs. Cunningham was the new teacher and she turned out to be my most favorite teacher. Fifth grade was great! Mrs. Altman was the sixth-grade teacher.

Mrs. Matthews' 3rd and 4th grade

Weda – 4th Grade

Chapter 21

Mrs. Cunningham, my Fifth-Grade Teacher

At the end of fourth grade, Mrs. Matthews tried to prepare us for fifth grade. There was a new teacher hired for fifth grade and no one knew her. Miss Cunningham lived in Fort Smith, Arkansas. She moved there to live with her mother and help take care of her. Everyone thought since she lived in Fort Smith and drove a long way - thirty miles - she was like a foreigner.

I'll never forget the first day of fifth grade. Miss Cunningham met us at the door with a smile. She made everyone feel so at ease.

First, she said, "We are going to learn a lot this year, but how can we learn in this drab classroom? Everyone looked around as if seeing the room for the first time. I thought, *Well, this looks like all the other classrooms*, which suddenly it hit me in my mind, *well, all the classrooms are drab!*

She said, "the first thing we are going to do is paint our desk tops." The desks were the ones with seats attached and room under the desk top for your books. "Everyone decide what color you want your desktop and tell me."

When we came back to school after the weekend, she had every desk top painted with the color each student chose. With the help of Mr. Wallace, the janitor, she painted most of the walls. What a bright cheery room it was. Everyone was so excited, and it made the class want to learn from a teacher who cared so much.

That year, I learned so much for I did not want to disappoint Miss Cunningham. I learned to read and memorize poems. I became interested in doing my homework as soon as I got home from school. This surprised mom so much that she went to school to meet this teacher that had changed my attitude toward school. Back then there was no meet-the-teacher night.

Right away, mom and Miss Cunningham hit it off, and mom became a home room mother. It wasn't long until a lot of other moms became homeroom mothers. Mom was the head home room mother and she would organize what the other mothers could do. Then, a homeroom mom was one that came on holidays to bring the treats, which back then were all homemade.

That year, I took the mumps and had to miss two weeks of school. Miss Cunningham sent me cards. After a week of being absent she drove out to our house, which was out in the country, with the work I had missed. She cared for her students and loved them. Since she had changed my attitude so much about school, that is when I first

thought about being a teacher when I grew up.

That school year ended too quickly. Mom and the other homeroom mothers made Miss Cunningham a patchwork skirt. This was during the time when piecing quilts by hand was done and then some made patchwork skirts from the material left over when the quilt was finished. This skirt idea started when you didn't have enough material to make a skirt, but you could sew all your leftover scraps to make a skirt. On each block, each student's name was embroidered.

I'll never forget the last day of school. Mom and the other homeroom mothers gave it to her. My mom and Miss Cunningham both started crying and the whole class started cheering.

Years later, after all Miss Cunningham's students had grown up, and she had retired, and all the students had gone to different areas of the states with jobs and raising their families, the skirt was forgotten.

Then one day I was with my brother Ray and we started down memory lane, and I remembered the skirt mom had put together for Miss Cunningham. We both said we wished we could find it and Miss Cunningham.

Years passed. One day, my brother called me and said Miss Cunningham's skirt had been found. It was bought from an antique shop by Michael Hightower who was younger than I. The news was put in the newspaper and my brother saved it for me.

My brother traveled to where we grew up for he was only about a two-hour drive away and he tried to buy the skirt for me. By then the skirt had been placed in our school museum, and they would not sell it at any price. I was sad, for I wanted that skirt so badly. My brother cheered me up by saying, "Look at it this way - it will be preserved in the museum long after we are gone, and our mom and Miss Cunningham will be remembered for a long time." I guess he is right, but I still want it and to be able to hold it, but I know it is in a safer place.

Through the years, I thought of Miss Cunningham a lot. After having two kids and while they were small, I went back to school to get my teaching degree. My first teaching job was in the library and then kindergarten. When I started teaching in the classroom I would think of Miss Cunningham and would decorate my room with bright colors. I would also stay in at recess to help students who were having a hard time with their work or insecure about school. I got criticized a lot by the other teachers telling me I was crazy to give up my recess. The principal and I had long visits about this and he said, "I wish more teachers showed the interest that you do." This interest did not come from my education classes in college, it came from remembering how insecure I was and a

teacher who helped me get over it by giving up her

recesses.

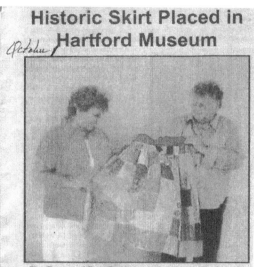

Historic Skirt Placed in Hartford Museum

Zina Rosso and Betty Penninton look over the skirt that was sent by Mary Ellen (Hightower) Britt to be placed in the Hartford Museum.

The skirt was made for Mrs. Juanita Cunningham by several volunteers and include the names of the Midland 4th and 5th grade classes at that time. The students whose names were embroidered on the skirt were Nancy Jane Rhodes, Loreida Schlinker, Martha Stangeland, Pauline Metcalf, David Bailey, Jimmie Ray Ervin, Charles King, Ana Mae Hearron, Dicy Louise Sutter, Jimmy emery, John Sharp, Thyrel Lovell, Jimmy Mody, J.W. Dugan, Nancy Sharp, Mrs. Faires–Room Mother, Jimmie Roy Thompson, Billy Howard, Brenda Sue Sutter, Walter King, Glen Cumbie, Mrs. Sutter–Room Mother, Brenda Altman, Mary Lee Repass, Jimmy Ray Cook, Eula Lee Cantrell, Lenora Barnes, weda Faires, Enna Dean Lovell, Janette Orr, Mary Ellen Hightower, Marilyn Douglas, Mable Pettus, Robert Presson, Mrs. Derrick–Room Mother, Bobby Derrick, Joe Smothers, Sandra Morrison, Judy Jensen, Barney Joe Ledbetter, and Edma Mae Escalante.

The Skirt

The Hightower family has reunion every year the weekend after Memorial Day at Tenkiller State Park, Oklahoma. To pay most of the expenses we have an auction each year to pay for the next. This year my brother, Michael, brought this skirt he had acquired. Obviously I didn't want it to be put in the auction and take the chance someone else would want it. I wrote Sherry a letter to ask if I could donate it to the Hartford Historical Museum, but before I did that I wanted to get Mike's story. The following is what I received in answer to my inquiry:

"I acquired the skirt last fall. A woman named Wanda Wasson has been in the antiques business in Fort Smith for many years, in various locations around the city. Most recently she has had a shop in the 100 block of North 3rd street, just off Garrison Ave. Last fall, she had a stroke and is no longer able to run the shop. A friend of mine, Dan Miller, and some other friends of hers were operating the shop for her, selling off as much as they could in

See The Skirt on pg. 2

preparation for closing the shop. One day, Dan called me and asked if I had a sister named Mary Ellen. I told him that I did, and he asked me if she had gone to school in Midland. Again, I said yes. Then he told me about the skirt, that it was in the shop, and said he thought I might be interested in it. Of course I was, very much, and asked him to hold it for me. A couple of days later he brought it into my shop, and I paid him $25 for it.

I have no idea where the skirt has been all these years, or how Wanda acquired it. I assume it came from an estate sale or garage sale, was bought by an antiques scout and then sold to Wanda. Wish I could tell you more." To be honest, I don't remember anything about it, but I am pretty sure the makers were Vivian Sutter, Juanita Derrick, and Weda Faires' mother, whose first name I cannot recall. I think it is a skirt they made for Mrs. Juanita Cunningham, who was the 4th-5th grade teacher. For those that cannot see all the squares on the skirt, there is one that has Midland, one with 4th & 5th grade, one with 1953-54, and a square for each person who was in those grades that year.

I would be very interested to know if anyone remembers it or has a tale to tell concerning it.

–Mary Ellen Hightower Britt
Memphis TN

See back page for more pictures of The Skirt! Perhaps you'll see your name.

Weda in 5th grade

(first time to have my hair cut short)

Chapter 22

Mrs. Altman 6th Grade

There is not a lot I remember about 6th grade. I remember Mrs. Altman was a quieter person and was very professional, but to me she was more an introvert. I mean by that it was hard to get close to her.

Brenda Altman was her daughter and we became good friends. Brenda said she didn't like her mother being the teacher for she thought her mother was too hard on her, harder than on the other students.

I got to know Mrs. Altman a little better for sometimes I got to go home with Brenda after school to play. She was more relaxed at home and always fixed us good after school snacks.

About the only thing I remember in 6th grade was my first boyfriend and the time I got in trouble.

I hated spelling and I hated studying for the spelling test. One night while studying spelling and mom was giving me the words to spell, I ask mom where she got the spelling of my name.

Mom told me I was named after her best friend, but she had changed the spelling of my name. My name is a French name and is supposed to be spelled Ouida. Mom said she thought she would spell it like it sounded, Weda.

Well I kept thinking about that and I told one of my friends that I thought I would put the spelling of my name Ouida on my spelling test paper. My friend warned me saying "that would be fun to see how Mrs. Altman would react but if you do you will get in big trouble!"

"No, I won't for she won't know who did it!"

Dumb reasoning from a 6th grader, who just hated studying for spelling

So, the night before the test I felt so good about what I was going to do, so I didn't study. I rode my bicycle and played until bed time.

The next day when time for the spelling test my friend who sat behind me said "You are not going to do it, are you"?

"Oh yes I am for she will never know who it is!"

I felt so confident as the spelling words were given.

When Mrs. Altman gathered up the papers she always looked to see if she had them all from the students. We were to read as she graded the papers.

Suddenly the class heard a sigh and a groan, then Mrs. Altman said, "Who is this?" She started trying to pronounce Ouida. "Is this Udah or Oda, and who in the world is this?"

By then the class was laughing for my friend had whispered what I had done.

Well by process of elimination Mrs. Altman figured out it was me. I had to go to her desk and tell her why I did it. She said you will stay in at recess for the rest of the day and write your spelling words over and over. She said, "I will also send a note home to your parents!" She was quiet for a moment then she begins to smile and said, "That is very interesting about your name, and I do like the spelling of it in French!"

Well I did get in trouble at home I had to do double on my chores and no play time. Mom for several weeks made me write my new spelling words over and over, and the correct way she spelled my name over and over.

I hated not getting to play and writing my spelling words so many times, but it was worth it in the end for it's still so plain to me even now Mrs. Altman's face and her trying to pronounce Ouida.

Mrs. Altman 6th Grade Class

Chapter 23

First Notice of Boys

I started to grow up in the way of noticing boys.

My first boyfriend was Aaron Dee Stanquist, whom I did not notice until Valentine's Day. He gave me a fancy valentine with a box of chocolates asking me to be his girlfriend. I was surprised, for he was shy, but he was very smart.

I didn't like the rich chocolates that came in a valentine box, so when I got home I showed mom the pretty card and gave her the chocolates. I thought mom would get on to me for having a boyfriend. Instead mom said, "You can sure have him for a boyfriend if you'll bring me the chocolates he buys for you!" Mom loved chocolates and our family could not afford them.

Aaron Dee and I stayed friends on into seventh grade. He was so shy that he didn't play with the rest of us. He usually just played with one other boy. Aaron Dee was smart and would help me with my homework. I think I was just too wild for him, for I had finally started enjoying school.

In seventh grade, we drifted apart.

J.W. Dugan wrote me a note, which was done a lot during that time. He wanted me to be his girlfriend. We were already playing together a lot and our parents were friends.

The teachers in seventh and eighth grade were Mrs. Rae and Mr. Carol Plunkett. Mr. Plunkett was the principal and I just loved him. Now Mrs. Rae was opposite. As I look back, the boys would test her patience, which she was short of, and us girls followed along.

After growing up and looking back, she was probably not that bad. After all, we were seventh and eighth graders.

J.W. And I remained girlfriend and boyfriend until about the middle of ninth grade. Even in eleventh grade after I had started dating Jimmie (my husband,) I thought I would like to go back to J.W.

We were riding the bus home from school when I made my desire known. I will never forget our conversation. J. W. said, "No, I want us to be friends forever, but Jimmie is a good man and you two go to the same church which I'll probably never do."

I cried some, but he consoled me and said, "Remember we are friends for life." He remained true to that statement, and I did, too, for there was always a special place in my heart for him and his parents who I loved dearly.

Chapter 24

My Baptism

I grew up going to the church of Christ. We went to several small churches in the area where we lived.

One reason we traveled back and forth to these small churches, was because my dad was a song leader. Dad came from a family that were singers. So, when the small churches needed a song leader they would call on dad. Some of the small churches we went to were Valley View Church of Christ on a dirt7 road between Midland Arkansas and Greenwood Arkansas. This church had a cemetery around it and a lot of large shade trees. This is where my mom and dad are buried.

Then we went to church at Midland Arkansas for a while. From there we went to Cameron, Oklahoma. The next church was Valley View Church, again only this time they had changed locations. The church was moved to Highway 10 which made it closer to Greenwood Arkansas.

Preachers talked of hell more then and hell was emphasized more than I think it is today. The question was always asked, "Don't you want to do right so you can go to heaven or go to hell where it burns forever?"

This got my attention and I started listening more each time I was at church. I also knew my mom and dad believed this for they lived by it each day, or I should say it was always on their minds. They read and studied their Bible. Dad could not read well for he only finished the 3rd grade. My mom was an excellent reader, so lot of nights mom read the Bible to dad.

As a child, I would be in bed supposed to be going to sleep, when I would hear mom and dad discussing the Bible. There were times it even turned into an argument. Since my dad was a poor reader he would take so many scriptures out of context. A lot of times dad was not looking at the scripture to apply to himself, but with the intent to prove someone else wrong. I went to sleep many nights with them discussing the Bible.

When I was ten years old, I started asking more questions, and I started becoming more scared that if I died I would go to hell. I started praying this little prayer that everyone knew at that time, or especially kids. I'm not sure who taught it to me.

Bedtime Prayer

Now I lay me down to sleep,

I pray thee, Lord. my soul to keep.

If I should die before I wake,

I pray thee, Lord, my soul to take.

One summer evening mom and Mrs. Williams were shelling peas to can. Mrs. Williams was our neighbor, who, along with her husband, went to the new Valley View Church. I approached the subject of being baptized. I knew several in my Bible class had been talking about being baptized. I'll never forget how Mrs. Williams put her arm around me and talked to me about it. She said, "If that's what you want, and it would help you to sleep better at night, then that's what you should do." I told her I was scared to go up in front of all those people at church, but she reassured me.

Now here's where the catch was - that I have thought about a lot. I feared water. I had never been in water over my head. I cried when mom would wash my hair. If water got into my eyes or ears, it scared me. Mom knew this, dad knew, and Mrs. Williams did. Knowing this, why didn't someone prepare or practice with me putting my head in water. All dad said in preparation was, "don't worry, the preacher will put a handkerchief over your nose and you will be fine."

Well, Wednesday night came and I along with three others from my Bible class went to the front of the church building to be baptized. Since three of my friends were going to be baptized, that made it easier for me to go to the front, for I wasn't alone.

Well, I about strangled to death and nearly drowned the poor preacher plus scaring him. The preacher thought everyone had been in water over their heads and he did not realize that I was that scared. My friends went first, and they did fine. I was sick a few days afterward due to swallowing a lot of water. Days later, after I recovered, I was one happy child, for now I was a Christian and could sleep better at night.

NOTE - Years later I had my husband re-baptize me. I wanted a baptism that was without fear of water. By then my husband had taught me how to swim, for he grew up without fear of water. He and his friends played in the creek all the time and he was an excellent swimmer.

Also, Mrs. Williams became a mother-in-law to Betty, my husband's sister.

Chapter 25

The Way We Said it in Arkansas

In Arkansas, I grew up with a lot of sayings. These sayings helped build character, pointed out other's mistakes, or just stated what we needed to be doing. Some were even medical advice, and some were superstitions.

When I didn't write on both sides of the paper, or left food on my plate, dad would say, "Waste not want not!"

If someone talks too much, mom would say, "She's got the gift of gab," which was not a compliment.

My dad whistled a lot when he was doing the farm chores. I practiced and practiced whistling. One day while helping mom can vegetables out of the garden, I started whistling. Mom said, "stop that whistling, girls are not to whistle." "Why?" I asked. Remember "Whistling girls and crowing hens will always come to some bad end."

When mom was not around, I would whistle, and I never came to a bad end. When I got older I asked my grandma, dad's mom, about whistling, and she said, "It's just not ladylike to whistle."

There were several cemeteries in the area where I grew up. I used to count the cars going to the cemetery after a funeral. Mom heard me counting one time and said "Stop! Never count cars going to the cemetery or you will be the next one to be buried." Of course, that was just a superstition, but it did make me stop counting the cars.

Heap coals of fire on one's head was used in our household as a Christian duty. If someone did you wrong, return good for evil. I argued with my parents saying, "Why should I treat them good after they have wronged me?" I didn't get anywhere with my argument for my parents would say "That's in the Bible, Proverbs 25:21-22."

My sister and I got caught telling a lie to dad and we tried covering it up by making excuses. Dad said, "You two are trying to wiggle out of this lie, just like a cat dancing on a hot tin roof."

I was told over and over that, "an idle mind is the Devil's workshop."

My parents and my in-laws were best friends, so I was in their house a lot while growing up. Now my husband, Jim, is five years older than I am so he was usually playing with his friends or somewhere else most of the time. I grew up knowing a lot of my mother-in-law's sayings. One of my favorites was when the bread or cake was not rising like it was supposed to. I would say, "What happened to the cake? It's flat." "Oh, it squatted to rise but cooked on the squat."

Mom and dad would say when wanting me to hurry with a job, "Hurry, we can get this done in two shakes of a lamb's tail."

When I tried to impress someone, dad would say, "Sis, you're getting too big for your breeches!"

After a good meal my dad would say, "Oh, that was so good. I'm as full as a tick!" This refers to what we called the dog tick.

I can still hear mom say when paying the bills, "Well, I have to rob Peter to pay Paul." Which means an unexpected bill came up and had to be paid immediately, so she had to take the money that was to be used for one bill to pay the unexpected bill.

When it was raining a downpour, what we called it in Arkansas, dad would say, "It's raining cats and dogs."

A thunder shower on a hot summer day with the sun shining meant two things. One, "the devil is whipping his wife" or, "it will rain again this time tomorrow." Rain again the next day happened a lot, but I'm not sure about the devil.

When we would visit our friends, and would be leaving they would say, "Come back to see us." Dad's response was, "Don't look for us until you see us coming."

Mom and dad, in describing some one that was very poor, would say, "He's as poor as Job's turkey." I never understood that saying until I got older and heard the Bible story of Job and how Satan had taken all his possessions. But I still wondered if Job even had a turkey. This saying really describes how poor in body the turkey was from lack of food.

People thought I didn't talk much and I didn't when out in public. A comment was made to mom,

"Your daughter is so sweet but very shy, she never talks." "Oh, yes, she does, she can talk the horns off a brass monkey when we are home."

We expressed surprise or shock by "Dear Me!" "My stars!" "Land sakes alive!" and "Not on your tintype!" When I was older, I started saying "Well, shuck my corn!"

Something that was to be a secret for a while, "Don't spill the beans!"

When dad wanted me to hurry doing the chores, he would say "Hurry, we're burning daylight!"

When you had company and they stayed past your bedtime, my dad and grandpa would say,

"Well it's getting past my bedtime, so would you please turn out the lights when you leave."

One that stuck with me that my grandpa, dad's dad, would use was, "It's 9:30, I'm home and I wish you were." No one took offence for everyone knew grandpa went by the clock. He was an early riser, up by five o'clock. If you spent the night at his house and you were not up at five o'clock, he would make a lot of noise by throwing and dropping his shoes on the floors to wake you up. There was no carpet then.

Dad was a fast worker and was always cheerful while doing his work. He was a coal miner, milked cows, goats, helped mom in the garden, and raised a lot of field crops. He plowed the ground with a team of mares, no tractors. When mom would get worried about him, she would say, "Grady, slow down and take a break!" His response, "I'd rather wear out than rust out."

Growing up hearing and using a lot of these sayings made me who I am today. Most of these sayings stated what real life is about. For example, I didn't want to be like the person who was as crooked as a barrel of snakes. Instead I learned in life that sometimes you had to take the bull by the horns and develop courage to face an unpleasant situation or to stand up for yourself.

More Sayings

Don't spill the beans (keep a secret).

To have a bone to pick (explaining or try to settle something disagreeable).

To be caught with one's pants down (to be taken by surprise, or unprepared).

Get down to brass tacks (get to the bottom of a thing).

Eager beaver (being persistent in a job and work like a beaver).

To eat crow (to take something back that was said wrong).

Face the music (face the consequences of something you did wrong).

To fly off the handle (to lose one's self control suddenly, just like the head of the ax could fly off suddenly and hurt someone).

To give a lick and a promise (is to not do the job thoroughly). Mom used this a lot when we didn't have time to clean the house, she would say, "Let's give it a lick and promise to do it better tomorrow."

To split hair (was to argue endlessly over something trivial).

To bury the hatchet (this goes back to an Indian custom).

In the nick of time.

Get off your high horse.

By hook or crook.

Jump out of the frying pan into the fire.

My husband when describing someone that looked unsightly he would say, "They looked like the hind wheels of hard times."

Lick your calf over (You do your job over - didn't do it right the first time).

That was better than I intended to do (Something turned out better than you thought it would).

I may add more sayings later, for I keep thinking of more, I just didn't realize we said so many until I started writing them down.

Chapter 26

Uncle Johnny

Uncle Johnny was another memory, for he was a fun-loving person. He was my dad's brother-in-law, married to his sister, Zelma, and he was my mom's uncle. Now, I was told how he was my mom's uncle, at the time it seemed too complicated to remember. I was more interested in how Uncle Johnny and Aunt Zelma's children were kin from both sides of the family. We kids thought we were double-kin, in our words.

The summer I was six, we were in Lancaster, Texas for our summer visit. Uncle Johnny was left in charge of me for some reason. It was a very hot day and Uncle Johnny said, "Have you ever had an ice cream cone?" "No," I said. "Well let's go buy one." We went to a Dairy Queen and he bought us two of the biggest ice cream cones, or so It was to me.

Well, I did not know how to tackle it, the only ice cream I had was in a bowl and it was homemade ice cream. Homemade ice cream has a different texture. Uncle Johnny saw my confusion. He started showing me how to lick my ice cream around and around, then how to eat my cone.

It was hot, and the ice cream was melting fast, so I was quite a mess by the time we finished our ice cream cones. After Uncle Johnny cleaned me up, I gave him a great big hug and said, "Thank you, that was very good!" He said, "Well, save your nickels and we will buy another one." That was what an ice cream cone cost then.

Since the ice cream cone was so good, I wanted mom to have one. I told Uncle Johnny my thoughts. The next day he took mom and me for an ice cream cone. He told us not to tell all the other cousins, for this was his surprise for mom and me. To this day, every time I eat an ice cream cone I think of Uncle Johnny and the special treatment he gave me in showing me how to an eat an ice cream cone. Years later, after I was grown and had kids, I thought of Uncle Johnny. I taught them to eat an ice cream cone the way Uncle Johnny taught me. I also told them the story of who taught me how to eat an ice cream cone. You may think this was no big deal, but everyone in the family talked about how Uncle Johnny could eat an ice cream cone so neatly.

Uncle Johnny and Aunt Zelma

Chapter 27

Uncle Bill and Uncle A.J.

Uncle Bill and Uncle A. J. were two of my favorite uncles and two funniest uncles.

They were mom's brothers. Every summer they would come to see us. They lived in California, not sure which city for they did move around a lot.

Uncle Bill owned a dry cleaner business and Uncle A. J. worked with him most of the time, when he wasn't doing construction work.

You never knew what to expect each year from Uncle Bill. He might show up with a wife, for he remarried many times, or he would show up with the back seat pulled out of his car and the back loaded with hound dogs.

Both uncles loved to hunt and fish, but Uncle A.J. didn't invest that much in hound dogs. He would have one, but it would be one not three to four hound dogs like Uncle Bill. Mom would get mad at Uncle Bill for bringing so many dogs that had to be tied to a tree in the back yard. The dogs would howl, which would get Rusty going, then that would scare the chickens, cows and goats, and sometimes ended in a fight among the dogs. The fight would end when a bucket of water was thrown on them. With that commotion going on, the chickens wouldn't lay as good and sometimes it affected how much milk we got from the cows.

I can still hear mom saying, "Bill, you've got to get rid of those dogs while you are here, for I want you to stay for a visit, but not the dogs." Uncle Bill would come up behind mom and hug her and say all kinds of sweet things to convince mom to let his dogs stay. It worked. They stayed.

Uncle Bill was a very handsome man dark hair, dark eyes, dark thin mustache. He looked like Clark Gable in *Gone with the Wind*. He could talk a person into anything. He was a very good story teller. I could listen to him and Uncle A.J. for hours telling their stories, some true and most not. Uncle A.J. Was shorter than Uncle Bill and had light red hair and a mustache and usually a dress cowboy hat.

There was something about Uncle A.J that drew me closer to him in a lot of ways. I noticed mom seemed to feel the same way. He cared for your feelings and I think at times he was just like a big teddy bear to me. Both my uncles not only were good storytellers, but they were good actors. They both had a small part in a movie or two, but I don't remember which ones. Mom didn't want them to talk about it, for she did not want them to become movie stars. Becoming a movie star was their goal and is why they were in California. Uncle Bill really wanted it worse than Uncle A.J., and I think mom talking to him a lot kept him from pursuing it. Aunt Jewell, A.J.'s wife, discouraged him. They were both very talented and the family thinks they would have succeeded, but with all the discouragement from everyone, they did not pursue it.

On one visit mom wanted to go to Fort Smith, which was about 30 miles from us, to do a little shopping at Woolworth, McCoy, and Kresses. These were called "5- and 10-cent" stores in those days. Uncle Bill said he would drive us there. When we were parked close to the stores, both uncles turned to mom and me and said, "We are going sight-seeing around, but if you see us, you act like you don't know us."

I thought that was so funny. True to their word, when mom and I were out on the street going to the next store, we met Uncle A.J. and he did not acknowledge us in any way. He had put on a different hat and fake sideburns and big sunglasses. I laughed so hard, but was also mad at him for not speaking. When we got home he explained to me that's what an actor is, pretending to be someone else. He knew I was hurt because he didn't speak to me.

It became a joke in mom's family, for at the Vincent Family Reunion everyone would say, "Wonder what new wife will Bill have this year?" Vincent was mom's maiden name.

The sad thing about both of my uncles is the fact that they could not leave alcohol alone. That got them in trouble a lot - job wise.

Uncle A.J., unlike Uncle Bill, had only one wife. Aunt Jewell and she was a Jewel in more ways than one. She and Uncle A.J loved each other but when he went on a drinking spell she wouldn't let him come home. Uncle A.J. understood that and amazingly respected it. Aunt Jewell worked also to help support herself when Uncle A.J. lost his job due to his drinking. She was also a good artist. I have two of the pictures she painted and one that Wanda, my sister, gave to me at her death. Jewell and I wrote letters back and forth to each other for years and she also wrote to mom a lot. They both wanted children but could never have any, so Aunt Jewell sort of adopted me.

When my dad started building the new house, Uncle A.J. was without a job. He came and stayed several months - not sure how long - to help dad build the house. Uncle A.J. was a good carpenter. Mom and dad had told him that he was not to drink while staying with them. He didn't drink while staying with us. He had quit several times before, and sometimes for long periods of time. Mom always thought Uncle Bill was Uncle A.J.'s weakness.

My uncles gave me a lot of laughter while I was growing up, especially Uncle A.J. When Jim and

I got married, he wrote a song especially for us. Both uncles were very good, music-wise, and they could play different instruments. They bought a lot of joy to mom; that's when I would see mom laugh the most. My dad just tolerated them. Uncle A.J.'s real name was Abner James. Uncle Bill's was William Henry.

I will always remember these uncles who brought a lot of laughs in this lonely girl's life.

Uncle A.J.

Uncle Bill and Wife

Chapter 28

Uncle Horace and Aunt Nellie

Another memory was Uncle Horace and Aunt Nellie who lived in Lancaster, Texas. In the summer, they would come to see us. They were my double cousins but since they were way older than me, I was to call them uncle and aunt. Mom felt sorry for Aunt Nellie because she wanted to have children but could never have any. Aunt Nellie loved all the cousins, nieces and nephews and she was loved back. All the kids loved going to their house.

The summer I was ten years old, I think, Aunt Nellie and Uncle Horace were visiting us. When they started to leave, they begged mom and dad to let me go home with them for a week. I was so excited, because I had not been far from home by myself.

One night, Aunt Nellie said, "Horace, let's go get a frosty root beer, for it's so hot." She looked at me and said, "Have you ever had a frosty root beer?"

"No," I replied.

We went to an ice cream drive-in, and Uncle Horace ordered us all a frosty root beer in a frosty mug. I had never felt anything so cold and so good. I thought I was living it up and I couldn't believe Aunt Horace and Aunt Nellie would drink something with beer in it. I knew if mom found out that I had been drinking beer she would kill me. I also started wondering if this would get me drunk like my Uncle Bill or Uncle A. J.

Aunt Nellie sensed something was wrong for I had stopped drinking my root beer. I told her "Mom is going to kill me, and I don't want to get drunk." She started laughing, then Uncle Horace, they laughed so hard that they were crying. Aunt Nellie pulled me into her arms and explained that this was not an alcoholic drink. What a relief! I was happy for I really liked that root beer, and I finished it and was so glad I wouldn't get drunk.

Even now, when I would get a frosty root beer I would think of Uncle Horace and Aunt Nellie.

Uncle Horace and Aunt Nellie

Chapter 29

My Mom

It's hard to write about mom for she was so many things. Mom was a very good cook and took pride in her cooking and setting the table right. Good housekeeper and organizer. Loved gardening and growing flowers. Worked hard in canning food from the garden and raised chickens for eggs to sell. Loved to read, sew quilts and made all our clothes. Mom had a good imagination and loved to try to write poetry, which she did write some Bible-content poems. Mom loved reading poems and she collected them. Mom loved mysteries so at a young age she got me started on the Nancy Drew Books which were very predictable but were for the young readers. Mom could order these from the Sears Catalog, and I got two or three almost every Christmas.

Mom was barely five feet tall with black hair and brown eyes. Mom was a perfectionist, she felt if the house wasn't cleaned or your appearance was not to the best then it was a reflection back on her. In other words, you were a lazy person.

Mom could be so strict but when she let her guard down she could be so much fun. Mom loved teaching kids Bible Class. Mom would have the whole Bible Class over to her house now and then. Her class was not that large about, seven to eight children from the ages six to eight years of age. Those were fun times for me and I enjoyed mom's Bible Classes, for she seemed more relaxed with me and not like my mother. Mom was a good teacher, I didn't realize that until years later when I got in other classes that I had learned more in mom's classes than I did with the other teachers.

Mom was nervous about certain things. When we came into the house after being gone, she would have dad go into the house and check under each bed and look in the closets, which were just rods with curtains over them.

I did not realize how nervous she was until one time when my dad was working the night shift at the mines. My mom and I had been at the neighbors shelling peas and it became dark as we drove the three miles home, which mom didn't intend for that to happen and she got so nervous. When we parked the car, Mom said "Weda, when we go into the house you look under one bed and I will look under the other." We only had one bedroom with two beds. "Okay." I said. When we got in the bedroom, I yelled "Mom which bed do you want me to look under?" Boy, did I get into trouble, for Mom said, "if there had been any one under the bed they could have grabbed us!"

Years later, I learned why mom was very nervous every time she came into the house. My mom's father, Mac Vincent, was an alcoholic. All the kinfolk said my grandpa was a fun-loving man until he got paid, and then he got drunk. My aunt Zelma, dad's sister, said the alcohol would turn his personality around and he would turn mean.

Grandpa, when drinking, would go home and turn violent on my grandma, chasing her with a butcher knife and chasing his kids. When drunk, he would hide in places and then jump out for the attack. Grandpa would hide behind doors, in closets and under the bed. My mom being the oldest of six kids would run with her younger siblings and hide them in the toilet – the outhouse - and other places so grandpa couldn't find them. Mom said it was hard keeping the younger kids from crying or being quiet, and all the time worrying about her mother.

Mom and her dad were very close until she reached the age of eight. Grandpa started drinking more and mom had to become the protector of her siblings.

Mom never got over the hurt of her dad. Years later grandpa wanted to regain the closeness back for he bragged to everyone how much he loved Ethel Mae, my mom, and could depend upon her. He missed that closeness even more so as he got older. He wrote to mom for several years trying to regain that closeness, even after mom was married and had grown children. Grandpa had my uncles, Uncle Bill and Uncle A.J., talk to mom and tell her he had changed. I remember mom getting letters from him, and she would cry for days. When she finally told me the reason she was crying, I was probably about thirteen. I would say, "Mom, you need to forgive grandpa!" I wanted her to restore the closeness, for I wanted to visit my grandpa and get to know him. Even when my grandpa got old and sickly and in the nursing home he would ask the other kinfolk to get Ethel Mae to come see him.

I can never remember meeting him, but folks kept sending mom pictures of him. My brothers and sister went to see him while he was in the nursing home. They offered to come get me to go with them. I thought about going for I wanted to meet grandpa, but I couldn't get all mom's tears out of my mind or her hurt, so I declined. Years later I thought about it and wondering if I might have been the one to help them get back together but I don't think so. For after I experienced hurt from my own dad I could understand mom more. As a Christian I knew I had to forgive dad but could never be close to him again, and that's how mom was.

Mom could never get over the hurt and damage he had done to her heart. Mom also blamed her dad for her mom's early death.

My mom and dad lived in East Texas for a while after they got married, then they moved to New Mexico. This move was under doctor's orders. for dad kept getting pneumonia and the doctor wanted him in a dryer climate.

One place they lived was south of Albuquerque New Mexico. It was called The Bosque Farm which was a government project of the Department of Agriculture. It was called the AAA, or Agriculture and Adjustment Act of the 1930's and early 1940's. It was a dairy farm. It was while mom and dad lived here that Granny, Ludie Elizabeth Vincent, came to live in a little house about one hundred yards away from mom and dad's house. My granny was separated from grandpa then. I wish I knew the details of this separation, but I don't.

My granny washed and ironed for people to earn money. By now granny's health was bad due to the hard life she had lived, or at least this is what I was told. I'm not sure how long she was there with mom and dad on The Bosque Farm before she died. Mom said the doctor said she died from consumption, meaning then, a lung disease or tuberculosis. My Granny was only fifty-nine years old when she died, and I was only six months old. My mom's youngest sister, Aunt Katherine, was sixteen years old. Aunt Katherine lived with mom and dad until she was eighteen.

Since I was so young, I never got to know Granny, but my two brothers and sister got to know her, and they loved her and told me about her when I got older.

So, I grew up wishing things had been different with my mom's parents. I saw my mom shed many tears over her mom and dad.

Sometimes mom would be cooking or canning, and she would be singing the song *Rock of Ages* and crying at the same time. I asked mom why that song made her so sad, yet she'd keep singing it. Her reply was "That's a very good hymn and it was my mom's favorite song and we sang it together." I guess by singing it even though it made her cry, she felt close to her mom.

At times when mom was sad or in deep thought, she would write a poem.

Influence

My life shall touch a dozen lives, before this day is done.

Leave countless marks of good or ill, ere sets the evening sun.

So, this wish I always wish,

This prayer I ever pray,

Lord, may my life help other lives, it touches by the way.

INFLUENCE

My life shall touch a
dozen lines, before this
day is done
Leave countless marks of
good or ill,
ere sets the evening Sun
So, this wish I alway wish,
This prayer I ever pray,
Lord, may my life help
other lives, it touches
by the way.

Ethel Mae's Bible Study Class

Granny Vincent and Uncle AJ

Chapter 30

My Dad

"Sis, would you like to go to the Murphy's Store with me?" Boy, did I!

It was a special time for me to get to go with dad by myself. The Murphy's Store was three miles from our house. It was in a community called Slaytonville. The store was at the top of what was called Slaytonville Hill. It was a very steep hill and at the top was a cemetery and a church.

One reason it was fun to go with dad was because he broke the rules of what mom wanted. When dad had the money, he would buy a coke - back then it was in a bottle. Mom did not want dad to drink a coke for she said it is not good for you. Dad would get a coke and tell me not to tell mom. "This is our secret!" That made me feel so big, for dad and I had a secret that mom didn't know about. Now, I had to drink Orange Crush or Grape Nehi, and I can still remember how that pop - which we called it - was so good and cold on a hot summer day.

Now, one time I asked dad why he liked coke and what was different about it than my Orange Crush or Grape Nehi? Well, after some thought dad said, "I'll let you taste of my coke, but you must never tell mom." "Oh, I won't. I promise." "Now, Sis, coke is a little stronger and you need to take a small sip, for it could sting your nose." I thought, *well, if dad can drink it, so can I.* So, I took too large of sip and boy, did it ever burn my eyes, throat and I got a little strangled. It scared dad but I was soon okay, and I said, "Now I know why mom doesn't want you to drink coke."

Before we would leave the store, dad would buy mom a Hershey candy bar or a Three Musketeer, two of mom's favorites. If dad treated himself even against mom's orders he would still treat her. That was something I wondered about as a child, "Did dad treat mom to cover up his drinking a coke or would he have done it anyway?"

I loved how dad would put peanuts, apples, pears or cookies mom had made in his pockets before he did the chores. Mom and dad didn't have much money, but they made sure somehow that they got fruit. Dad would raise the peanuts and would get pears and apples off an old chiropractor that mom used. They would pick them on the halves - meaning they each got half - for the doctor did not have time to pick, so the fruit got picked and was not wasted.

Dad never complained about all the hard work and he was always whistling. He liked to tell jokes or make up jokes, but bless his heart some of his jokes were dumb and no one ever got the punch line.

Dad was helpful to others in need, sometimes to the point that he would get behind in his own work.

He knew music well, especially hymns; he could read shaped notes. He came from a family that liked to sing hymns. His sister, Zelma, had seven kids and they went as a family, singing at funerals and weddings or other occasions. Dad was a good song leader at church.

Dad had only a third-grade education, which amazed me how he could be a carpenter and build and measure the lumber. He could not read well, which frustrated him at times for he wanted to read the Bible. Mom helped him in his reading. At night after the work was done they would sit at the kitchen table working on dad's reading. The trouble was, as dad learned to read he had trouble getting the meaning of the words, which mom worked with him a lot. To me, dad would read more into the reading than was there, and he was always taking things out of context. But as I grew up I saw how important reading was by watching my dad learn under mom's guidance. He and mom would get in more discussions when he would read the Bible, for he could not stay in the context. I can still see mom, how aggravated she was. As an adult going to college to become a teacher, I really could see how dad missed out on not learning to read in context when he was young.

But dad never gave up and mom never gave up helping him, which I think shows the character of both parents.

Dad was not a good money manager. Mom did all the bill paying. Dad could not figure out how to spread the money around, like pay a little on each bill. One time he paid the bills, but what he did, he paid all the money he had on one bill, and didn't have any money left to pay some on the other bills or to buy groceries. So that's how mom ended up doing all the bill paying.

Dad was so good at building things or patching what we had. He made me several toys while growing up. He made me a doll buggy, a wagon made of wood, swings, doll beds, a whistle, a toy box and a cedar chest for us girls. He made mom a kitchen sink out of a gas tank from an old car. He ran a pipe from the sink to a ten-gallon bucket outside for the dishwater to run in. If mom was canning, he would put a tub or larger container outside and my job was to empty it by using a smaller bucket. We took the dishwater and watered the flowers with it. I remember several neighbors came by to see the sink, for no one had thought of or heard of doing this.

Dad was a hard worker. As I look back I wondered how he had the energy to keep going.

He farmed, plowed acres of land with just a mare or sometimes a team. He grew watermelons to sell, peanuts, field peas, field corn, feed for the cows. Baled hay and grew cane, which was later made into molasses. Mr. McConnell, a neighbor, had a sorghum molasses mill, and they would cook the molasses together. Dad would give him a percent of the molasses. Mr. McConnell had the big cooking pot and a horse or a mule that would walk in circles around the big pot to keep the molasses stirred.

Dad also helped mom in the garden, milked cows. The milk was sent to a creamery. He milked goats and worked as a carpenter. Then to top it off, he worked in the coal mines.

A lot of dad's friends and church friends had started working in the mines. Farming was the way of life in Sebastian County, where we lived, until the discovery of coal in the late 1800's.

Coal mining within the state of Arkansas began as open pits, called strip mining, but as time went on it turned to underground mining for greater efficiency. This underground mining followed the slope of the natural coal bed, gathering and extracting the coal as the slope shaft continued to follow the coal bed. Steel tracks would be laid, and the coal removed by coal carts pulled from the mine. That was also how most mines got the miners down in the mines in the coal carts.

One of the advantages of Arkansas coal is that it gives off little smoke when it burns. Also, it was low in sulfur and had a high carbon content which made it a more efficient fuel than coal in other parts of the United States.

Well, times were getting hard and money shorter. Dad had looked everywhere for some extra work, but there was none.

His friends kept saying, "Grady, try to get a job at the coal mines."

"Oh no!" my mother said. My grandma and grandpa, who were dad's parents, agreed. "That is just too dangerous!"

One night, Brother Major Glidewell, from the Midland Church of Christ, came to visit dad with the intention of getting him a job in the mines. Brother Glidewell worked in what we called the Bill Lewis Mines - named after Lewis - but the real name was the Peerless Mines at Greenwood, Arkansas.

I was either six or seven then and I will never forget that night.

"Grady, I will be by in the morning to pick you up to go work in the mines," Brother Glidewell said. My dad, with little hesitation, said, "Okay." My mom started crying and told Brother Glidewell to get out of the house and never come back.

Brother Glidewell said, "It's hard work, Grady, but once a coal miner, always a coal miner, for it gets in your blood." That ended up being true, for dad loved his coal mining buddies. You can see why. When you work side by side with another buddy in a space no higher than forty-five inches or less, you get to know that person well.

All the family worried about him and he got injured several times, with rocks falling on him. His left hand got permanent damage where he could not straighten three fingers on that hand, but he learned to continue to work even with that damaged hand.

Dad would come in several times with his dinner bucket squashed flat, but he would always say better the dinner bucket than me. Which always scared me for his dinner bucket was always by his side. Dad had to replace his dinner bucket many times. The dinner bucket had three compartments. Water was stored in the bottom. The center section held food and a tray on top to hold dessert.

The clothes the miner wore were overalls with long underwear underneath. They wore hard hats with a carbide light on top. There was a wash house that the miners washed in before coming home. When dad got home you could still see coal dust around his eyes. It looked like mascara.

Once a week, dad would bring his mine clothes home and mom would wash them several times, but you could never get all the coal dust out and she would hang them on the line. At least the clothes smelled better.

Dad loved the song *Sixteen Tons*, but mom hated it. The song was true because you did owe your soul to the company store.

Several of dad's friends died in the coal mines from cave-ins or explosions. Some died of rock dust on their lungs and then a lot with the coal dust settled on their lungs, which was called black lung disease. In later years, dad did get the black lung. I can remember him having pneumonia a lot. As the mines started shutting down due to lack of coal, dad was able to draw his black lung pension. My dad still lived to be eighty and one-half years old. A major heart attack put him in the hospital. Two or so years before, the doctor said having black lung made it hard on his heart, for the black lung was making him short of breath which made it hard on his heart. The doctor said it was amazing the black lung didn't kill him sooner.

At Greenwood, Arkansas, the Historical Society built a Memorial Park, that was dedicated on October 21, 2000 to honor local coal miners and their role in History. It features a coal miner statue (which was "Bud" Lewis, the owner of the mines that dad worked in.) There are two granite walls displaying names of miners from the county, and my dad's name is on this wall, along with my father-in law's name.

My dad was happy farming, working in the coal mines and going to small churches to lead the singing. My dad was a happy man until the day he got a call at work to come home for my mother had been killed in a freak car accident. Her own car ran over her.

Dad was never the same after that. He lived twenty years after mom's death. Dad did remarry, but he was never happy like he was with mom. Jim and I were with him when he drew his last breath and with him holding my hand, he looked at me and said, "Do not grieve, for I'm going home to Ethel Mae!"

Grady and Ethel Mae Faires

Chapter 31

Freak Accident

Mom and dad now lived in their new house that dad and Uncle A.J., my mom's brother, had built. This house set on forty acres not far from The Turner House. Dad and mom had saved for years and bought the forty acres, then saved and took out a loan to build the new house they had dreamed about for years. Uncle A.J. Stayed with us for several months to help dad build the house.

The house was so beautiful that mom wanted it to stay in the family long after she and dad were gone. Dad agreed, and mom wrote on paper that the house was to go to Jim and I and Aunt Jewell, Uncle A.J.'s wife, at one or both of their deaths. Mom showed me where she put the papers in her old black purse that was kept in the cedar chest.

To get to the house you turned off the main dirt road that was close to the Tyro Church building onto a one-lane road. The mailboxes set close to the turnoff and dad had put a wire gate across the one lane road, so the cows would not get out. Mom would open the gate, drive through, get out of the car, check the mail and then put the gate back up.

This day mom had called me, for we were living in Tahlequah, Oklahoma a little after noon time. Mom said, "Weda, why don't you and the kids come down for a few days?" I replied, "Mom, I will come down next week." "Ok, I will be looking forward to seeing Adonis and Alethea."

Adonis, our son, had just turned four years old and Alethea, our daughter, had just turned one year of age.

Mom finished the phone conversation by saying "I'm going to the little store and get some milk, for dad and I are going to have cornbread and milk tonight." The little store was on the corner of the dirt road.

That was the last time I heard mom's voice!

It wasn't but an hour or more, I'm not sure just how long, that my father-in-law called wanting to talk to Jimmie, which was what he called him. He wasn't interested in talking to me, which was very unusual. In my mind I thought, *how strange?*

He was calling to tell about mom, for she had been found under the car. It was evident how the accident had happened: she had driven the car through the gate opening and left the car idling in park. Her back was turned towards the car while she was shutting the gate. The car was idling too fast, or so the mechanic said later, so it vibrated out of park and rolled back fast, catching mom between the gate and the car, pulling her under the car. She was found soon by two teenage boys, but it was too late. Phone calls were made, and my father-in-law and other neighbors rushed over to lift the car off mom, hoping to revive her.

Well, during the next couple of months, we tried to help dad the best we could. Then he approached us and said he was getting married again. That was a shock to us all, for it was too soon after mom's death. Dad and his new wife, Lois, were going to continue to live in the house.

Not many weeks later Lois wanted to go back to her house in Poteau, Oklahoma. Then we heard dad was going to sell the house.

"What!" I said, "does he not remember the plan him and mom made after the house was built?"

After mom's death we were not financially able to buy the house, but Aunt Jewell was, and we were to pay her back. She had been wanting to come to the Midland area and retire to be close to us and our kids, who she adored. She had even bought some land off my father-in-law in Midland, Arkansas.

She was living in California and had promised Uncle A.J. that if something happened to him first, she would move back and be close to mom or us. She was now by herself, Uncle A.J. having died a few months ahead of mom.

Jim and I approached dad at the time he was going to remarry and move, to buy the house. Dad refused us and said he knew the house was promised to us with us paying for it if he moved. Well, in his words he said, "I will not sell it to you or Aunt Jewell." I was in shock. I even went back to dad the next day crying and saying, "Dad you won't be out any money for we will pay for it, and remember the promise you and mom made."

Dad became very harsh with me and said "No!" I couldn't believe it. Neither could Jim nor Aunt Jewell. My dad had never spoken that harsh to me. We went home to Tahlequah, Oklahoma, which was ninety miles from my dad's. I don't think I ever cried as hard, along with Aunt Jewell.

In discussing it with others, we found out later that Lois had a big influence over this. I even went to her, but got nowhere and found out that she did not care for our feelings. Because of this and other things I was never close to her or my dad after that.

Outside of house

Living room

Chapter 32

Grandpa and Grandma Faires

Grandpa and Grandma Faires

There is nothing like suddenly being awakened at five a.m. in the morning by a man's work shoe hitting the wall. That's the way grandpa would get you out of bed if you spent the night at his and grandma's house.

Grandma and Grandpa Faires were the only grandparents I knew. They lived in Lancaster, Texas for years, then later they moved to Seagoville, Texas to be close to Uncle Ruskin, my dad's brother, who also lived there. I knew grandpa loved his kids and grandkids, but he had certain rules or structures that you followed.

Sometimes we would spend the night with Uncle Ruskin and Aunt Willa Mae. On those nights we would visit with grandma and grandpa until their bedtime. Dad would tell grandpa as we were leaving their house to go to Uncle Ruskin's, "I will see you at eight in the morning, Poppa." Sometimes, the next morning, dad would run a few minutes after eight due to visiting with Uncle Ruskin, and the first thing grandpa would say was, "Grady, you are late," showing him his pocket watch.

Grandpa wanted everything to run on time. Grandma fixed the meals on time, or I should say, grandpa's time. Grandpa was a hard worker, so mom and dad told me, for by the time I came along, grandpa was retired and only did odd jobs. I do remember he raised peach trees and a garden.

I saw as a child that he at times made more work for my grandma. Grandma kept newspapers or old magazines at the end of the sofa. In helping grandma straighten the house up in the mornings, I picked the newspapers up and grandma said, "No, Weda, leave those there, for that's for when your grandpa comes in from working outside with muddy shoes." Grandpa would go to the sofa for a short nap and would not pull his muddy shoes off. I thought that was so thoughtless, and I said so to grandma. I will never forget what grandma said, "Yes, I could make a big fuss and we would end up in a big argument, so to avoid that and save dirt from getting on the sofa I just put newspapers there."

I learned so much from my grandma; she was one of the most patient women I've ever known. I remember after breakfast when the dishes done, grandma would go to the bedroom. She had a rocking chair in the corner and she would pick up her Bible and start reading. She would do the same thing before going to bed, no matter how tired or late that was. As I grew up watching my grandma do this I was impressed. As I got older and married I realized not only did grandma read the Bible, but she put it into practice every day.

It was amazing the work grandpa could get done. When he was young he lost his right hand and part of his arm in a saw mill. He had a stump of his arm below the elbow, but it was withered and smaller. Grandma would sew a white sleeve like a pocket for that arm to go into and grandpa would put a man's garter, that was used to hold up a man's sock, at the top. You never saw him without it, and it was always white.

In the early '50's, there was a drought which meant there had been no rain in a long time and the wells and streams of water were drying up. This was bad for dad since we had cows, goats, and chickens that needed water. Also, all the crops were dying and there was no hay to bale, so this meant a food shortage for the animals and us.

Way out in the woods there was a natural spring which dad found when we first moved to The Turner Place. The cows would find it at times and get a drink while grazing in the pasture. This spring had not dried up, but the water flowed into the spring slow and you had to drop your bucket deep to pull a bucketful up.

Grandma and grandpa had been writing and asking about the water situation. They even called several times, which you didn't do back then, for it was so expensive. Cell phones had not even been thought of.

Dad had found a place, I don't remember where, that he could take barrels and fill up with water and haul back to the farm on his old International truck. That was a job, for he had to fix a large container to pour the water in for the livestock to drink out of. Dad was getting worn down, working in the mines and coming in and hauling water plus all the other work that had to be done on the farm. Mom and I were getting worn out too. Mom taught me how to use the dish water twice and the rinse water several times.

Grandma and grandpa decided it was time for them to come help us. Uncle Ruskin brought them to our house. This happened while we were living at The Turner House. There was a little outbuilding close to the house that one part of it that was used to store the canned food. Dad built shelves for the fruit jars to sit on. It had a dirt floor and it was cooler in there. There was a larger room that connected to the outhouse, so when we moved there my brother, Ray, wanted to make that his room. Dad helped him put a floor in it and it had one window and a door. As time went by, mom helped Ray paper the wall and made curtains for the window. It turned out to be a very cute room. When grandma and grandpa came to help, my brother had already left home, so this was the room grandma and grandpa stayed in.

I loved it that grandma and grandpa were in that room. This was a time I got to know my grandpa better.

Since it was hard to lift a bucket of water from the spring, dad and grandpa put posts up like you do for a well and got a pulley with a rope to draw the water. Every afternoon, grandpa would draw water from the spring. When I would get off the bus from school I would get in my chore clothes. These were different than the clothes you wore to school or church. I would yell at Rusty if he wasn't with grandpa and head to the spring to help grandpa.

I remember surprising grandpa once, for he thought I was helping mom, and that was the first time I saw grandpa with his pocket sleeve off his arm. It embarrassed grandpa, and since I was just a kid, I was curious about it, but grandpa hurriedly put his pocket sleeve back on.

Grandpa and grandma stayed a month. At the end of their month, we started getting some rain and grandpa said, "It's time for us to go home." I was sad, for I had enjoyed them so much. Grandma had helped me start a quilt and grandpa had played little silly games with me. I don't remember what they were, but it was a side of grandpa I hadn't seen, and it was something I held in my heart.

After they left mom and I both wrote to them every week. Mom missed grandma so terribly much. We would go see them every summer and most Christmases.

Time moved on, and the year I was fourteen years old, I think, we were suddenly awakened in the middle of the night by the phone ringing. Dad answered the phone and he said, "Oh, no!" Mom

jumped out of bed and ran to dad's side. The call

was from Uncle Ruskin and grandpa had suddenly

died of a heart attack. That was the first time I saw

my dad cry.

After we got someone to take care of the

farm, we were on the road to Texas. It was an eight-

hour trip in a car with no air conditioning.

This was my first experience of seeing a

coffin in the house. Back then, the tradition was to

bring your loved one back to the house where

friends and relatives would come by to view the

body and visit with the family. Also, relatives took

turns sitting with the body. The body was never left alone day or night.

Grandma would put her arm around me and say, "Weda, come see your grandpa." Well, that scared me, for I had never seen anyone in a casket up that close, especially not grandpa. Grandma would reassure me and tell me that grandpa had gone to a better place. Grandpa's funeral was to be on a Sunday afternoon, so the casket stayed at the house until just before the funeral.

I will never forget that Sunday morning, everyone was worried about grandma. Dad and Uncle Ruskin and everyone else were in their church clothes and I heard them discussing who would stay with grandma while everyone went to church. Grandma said, "No one is to stay with me, for I'm going to church this morning." She said this as she was coming out of the bedroom. Everyone looked up and was so surprised, for there was grandma in the doorway looking pale, but in her church clothes.

Uncle Ruskin and dad said, "Mom, you need to rest and sat by poppa for it will be a long afternoon with the funeral."

Grandma said, "I can't do Lee (grandpa's name) any good now, so I best go to church like the Lord wants, so I can go to him." Everyone got real quiet, then someone said, "I will stay, while you go to church." I don't remember who it was, for I was like everyone else, so surprised about grandma leaving grandpa.

Grandpa's funeral was the first for me. My dad, Uncle Ruskin and Aunt Zelma and Uncle Johnny's family and maybe others did the singing. Most of grandma and grandpa's kids and grandkids did a lot of the singing, also. I remember the singing was beautiful, and there is one song they sung that I had never heard. It was called *Home of the Soul.* It has a base lead. It's been one of my favorite songs since that time.

After grandpa's death, grandma calmly, the best I can remember, went on with her life, never complaining. Mom and I wrote her a lot of letters and called more often. Every summer, I would go stay a week or more with her and those were the best times for me.

While visiting Grandma one summer, she gave me some material to sew a dress. I loved the material it had large pink dots. Grandma gave me some white material to trim the dress.

Grandma said, "This will make you a good church dress."

"No grandma I've been wanting a new dress for my date with Jim!"

Then I sighed, "Oh No!" "What's the matter?" said grandma.

"Well mom's sewing machine is broken right now!"

"Well what's the problem?" Grandma said, "You have two good hands to hand sew that dress!"

When I got home that's what I did. It took me longer probably a week with  mom's guidance, but I hand sewed the last stitch on Friday. Just barely made it in time for I had a date with Jim that night. I was so proud of that dress and I loved the dress. Mom took a picture for me to send to Grandma.

The summer I was seventeen years old, Jim, my husband, and I were dating, and we would write to each other several times a week while I was visiting grandma. Grandma one day said, "Weda, this must be serious, for you sure are getting a lot of letters from this Jim." I told her it was and then I told her a lot about Jim. I'll never forget grandma would say "Weda, marriage is serious, so be careful who you marry and make sure he loves God as much as you and that he's a sincere Christian." When I assured her that he was a Christian, she said, "Well, we need to get busy then, making you a quilt." I will always remember that quilt, for I sewed it by hand and the quilt had the pattern that is called "A Trip Around the World."

Grandma lived until I was married, and we had our first child, Adonis. When Adonis was three months old, we went with my mom and dad to see grandma. Grandma had been sick and in and out of the hospital a lot. She was diagnosed with skin cancer - melanoma. It soon got in her bones and she did not last long then.

Of course, I was sad, and mom was, also, for she was so close to grandma, her mother having died young.

Out of mom's grief, she wrote a poem.

In Memory of Mom Faires and Grandma Faires

Mother was fourscore years
Plus, weeks a few,
When she left us to go
live beyond the blue.

She must have been lonely
at times we know,
Dad having passed on
seven long years ago.

Yet she murmured not,
neither did she complain,
whatever her lot.
She was always the same.

We will miss her
from day to day,
Yet we cannot wish her back,

On this old earth to stay.

To be with the Lord
Is for better we know.
So, let us watch and pray,
And be ready to go.

Memories will live,
In our hearts on and on,
Of her courage, her
faith, so brave and strong.

May our lives ever be,
faithful and true,
So that someday too,
We may live beyond the blue.

Grandma & Grandpa Faires (wearing sleeve made by
Grandma Faires)

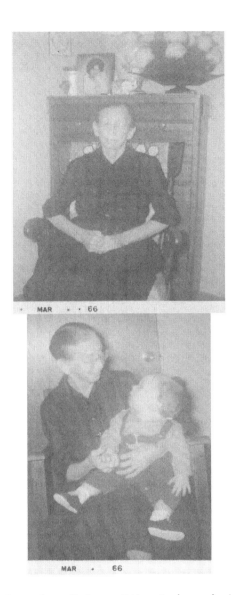

Grandma Faires sitting in her chair
Grandma Faires talking to Adonis (my son)

Chapter 33

My Quiet Place

Rusty was my dog, given to me by my brother, Ray. Ray thought this puppy would replace my Billy, the goat that he traded for the Victrola. He felt guilty, and although Rusty did not replace Billy, with mom's training he turned out to be the best and useful pet.

I fixed some peanut butter and crackers. Now, my way was to stack three or four crackers with peanut butter in between. I learned this from mom. Fix a quart jar of water, for it was hot, but mainly to wash the peanut butter and crackers down. There was a slight chance of getting choked.

Off to the woods Rusty and I went. I went to my favorite place where there were some pine trees and a big wild dogwood tree that was loaded with white flowers. I've never seen one that large since.

This place was a secret, it was way in the woods where the cows and goats did not wander. Mom and I found it by accident. We called it our quiet place. Only dad knew about it, years later we showed it to some others in the family, but not many, and they were not to tell. The pine needles fell under the dogwood tree which made the ground soft and clean and at times if the wind was just right you could hear the pine trees humming.

Finally, Rusty and I were laying on the pine needles. It was a beautiful hot, sunny day, with the clouds floating across the blue sky like puffy pillows.

I watched the clouds and thought about life. *Would I grow up and marry?* or *Would I get rich, so I could buy mom and me some pretty dresses?* I thought about my brothers and sister and wondered why they had to be older than me?

After thoughts and daydreaming, Rusty and I would have our peanut butter and crackers.

Sometimes I would fall to sleep, for it was so peaceful, with the birds singing. Sometimes mom would come with us and I loved these times. Mom would be more relaxed than at home and we talked and dreamed together. I learned a lot about my mom during these times.

Years went by and I continued to go to my favorite place during the warm weather. I was not allowed to go there without Rusty. He would kill copperheads or any snake or tarantula. I took my husband there after we married until we moved to Oklahoma. Also, today I'm thinking of that big dogwood tree and Rusty, wishing I could go back in time. Just thinking about it gives me pleasure of knowing that I had my own special quiet place with my buddy Rusty.

Even now, sixty years later for me, we all need our quiet place. But it can be hard to find one in this noisy society today. We are so connected to the outside world in so many ways now. Phones ringing, television on with the news, e-mails dinging on your phone, so we need to take control to be able to have a quiet time and a quiet place. I have made a quiet corner in my house to shut the world out for one hour in the morning, sometimes it is the sun room. It is hard nowadays to find your quiet spot, but do it and commit yourself to 1 hour. It may mean you have to get up earlier, which I am doing before the rest of the world wakes up.

I have made my quiet place a space in my own home. The advantage of having your quiet space in your home, is it will always be there. Go there each day and meditate, read and write.

My Quiet Place

Think of Psalms 23:

The Lord is my shepherd, I shall not want.
He leads me beside quiet waters.
He makes me to lie down in green pastures;
He leads me beside the still waters.
He restores my soul;
He leads me in the paths of righteousness for His
name's sake.
Yea, though I walk through the valley of the shadow of
death, I will fear no evil; For You are with me; Your rod
and Your staff, they comfort me.
You prepare a table before me in the presence of my
enemies;
You anoint my head with oil; My cup runs over.
Surely goodness and mercy shall follow me All the
days of my life; And I will dwell in the house of the
Lord Forever.